AF644467

"Contrary to some assertions that India's growth has been *jobless*, the Employment-Unemployment Surveys of the National Sample Survey Office, which till date remain the most reliable sources of information on India's employment situation, have consistently reported low and stable rates of unemployment over more than three decades. Even under the most demanding definition of employment, the unemployment rate consistently remains between 5 percent and 8 percent".

—NITI Aayog, *India: Three Year Action Agenda (2017-18 to 2019-20)*, August 2017, pp. 3-4.

Entrepreneurship, *Make in India* and Jobs Creation

P. Madhavi
Assistant Professor of Economics,
Department of Women's Studies,
Sri Padmavati Mahila Visvavidyalayam, Tirupati

and

G. Satyanarayana
UGC Emeritus Fellow, and formerly Dean of Social Sciences and
Director, Centre for the Study of Social Exclusion and Inclusive Policy,
Sri Krishnadevaraya University (S.K. University), Anantapuramu,
Andhra Pradesh

New Century Publications
New Delhi, India

NEW CENTURY PUBLICATIONS
4852 / 24, 1st Floor,
Ansari Road, Daryaganj,
New Delhi – 110 002 (India)

Tel.: 011-4101 7798; 4358 7398; 98112 66355
E-mail: info@newcenturypublications.com

www.newcenturypublications.com

Editorial office:
4800 / 24, Bharat Ram Road,
Ansari Road, Daryaganj,
New Delhi – 110 002

Copyright © 2018 by the authors

All rights reserved. No part of this book may be reproduced, stored in a retrieval system, or transmitted in any form or by any means, mechanical, photocopying, recording, or otherwise without the prior written permission of the publisher.

Reprint: 2024

ISBN: **978-81-7708-474-0**

First Published: 2018

Published by New Century Publications and printed at Milan Enterprises, New Delhi.

Designs: Patch Creative Unit, New Delhi.

PRINTED IN INDIA

About the Book

Entrepreneurship is the quality of being an entrepreneur, i.e. one who *undertakes an enterprise*. The term puts emphasis on the risk and effort taken by individuals who both own and manage a business, and on the innovations resulting from their pursuit of economic success.

National Policy for Skill Development and Entrepreneurship, 2015 aims to bring the world of education and training closer to the world of work so as to enable them together build a strong India. It provides clarity and coherence on how skill development efforts across the country can be aligned within the existing institutional arrangements. The policy links skill development to improved employability and productivity.

Make in India is an initiative of the Government of India to encourage multinational, as well as domestic companies to manufacture their products in India. It was launched by Prime Minister Narendra Modi on September 25, 2014. The objective is to make India as the top destination globally for foreign direct investment (FDI).

Presently, India is one of the youngest nations in the world with more than 62 percent of its population in the working age group (15-59 years), and more than 54 percent of its total population below 25 years of age. The problem of the educated unemployed raises special issues. It has to be tackled through proper educational planning and schemes of training, skill formation and entrepreneurial development.

This book provides a comprehensive account of policies and programmes for entrepreneurship development in India. More importantly, it details various programmes and schemes—including the flagship *Make in India* Campaign—of the Government of India to create jobs for the young population of India.

About the Authors

Dr. P. Madhavi is currently Assistant Professor of Economics, in the Department of Women's Studies, Sri Padmavati Mahila Visvavidyalayam, Tirupati. Earlier she worked as lecturer in JNTU College of Engineering, Anantapur. She obtained her M.A. Degree in Economics from Sri Krishnadevaraya University, Anantapur, Andhra Pradesh and was awarded the Gold Medal. She also received her M.Phil. and Ph.D. degrees from the same university. She has also published and presented 17 articles in journals and conferences. Her areas of interest include women empowerment, women entrepreneurship, and industrial economics.

Professor G. Satyanarayana is presently Emeritus Fellow of University Grants Commission (UGC) at Sri Krishnadevaraya University (S.K. University), Anantapuramu, Andhra Pradesh. He retired as Dean of Social Sciences and Director, Centre for the Study of Social Exclusion and Inclusive Policy from the same University. A Gold Medallist in M.A. (Economics), he has more than 100 research papers and 11 books to his credit. He successfully completed one major research project sponsored by the UGC, New Delhi. Earlier he worked as Director, College Development Council, S.K. University, Anantapuramu and also as a Senior Research Officer at the Centre for Planning and Development Studies, a Premier State-sponsored Research Centre in the University. Deeply interested in the economics of cottage and small-scale industries and environmental economics, he has produced 38 Ph.D. and 22 M.Phil. scholars in different areas of economic research. He was awarded the Andhra Pradesh State Best Teacher Award for the year 2010.

Contents

Preface

The growth and prosperity of all economies remains highly dependent on entrepreneurial activity. Entrepreneurs are the essence of economic growth as they provide a source of income and employment for themselves, create employment for others, produce new and innovative products or services, and drive greater upstream and downstream value-chain activities. Supportive environments are increasingly essential to successful entrepreneurship and these are evolving across the world.

The face of entrepreneurship is also changing. Across the world, entrepreneurs are increasingly young and/or female due to increasing unemployment. The public and private sector each have an important role to play in creating entrepreneurial ecosystems that, in addition to funding, are essential to promoting entrepreneurial success.

Developed economies generate entrepreneurial opportunities as a result of their wealth and innovation capacity, yet they also offer more wage employment options to attract those that might otherwise become independent entrepreneurs. If these opportunities for entrepreneurship and innovation are to be captured, it is essential to create an enabling eco-system for entrepreneurship to thrive and instil a mind-set and culture of opportunity and innovation-based motives and entrepreneurial incentives.

Entrepreneurship has been considered the backbone of economic development. It has been well-established that the level of economic growth of a region, to a large extent, depends on the level of entrepreneurial activities in the region. The myth that entrepreneurs are born, no more holds good. Rather, it is well-recognised now that the entrepreneurs can be created and nurtured through appropriate interventions in the form of entrepreneurship development programmes.

In the era of liberalisation, privatisation and globalization along with ongoing IT revolution, capable entrepreneurs are making use of the opportunities emerging from the evolving scenario. However, a large segment of the population, particularly in the industrially backward regions/rural areas generally lags behind in taking advantage of these opportunities. Therefore, there is a need to provide skill development and entrepreneurship development training to such people in order to bring them to mainstream of economic growth.

Entrepreneurship development programmes (EDPs) are being organized in India as a regular training activity to cultivate the latent qualities of youth by enlightening them on various aspects that are necessary to be considered while setting up enterprises. These programmes are conducted generally for technicians/artisans for motivating them towards self-employment. The course contents of such EDPs are so designed as to provide useful information on:

- Product/process design.
- Manufacturing practices involved.
- Testing and quality control.
- Selection and usage of appropriate machinery and equipments.
- Project profile preparation.
- Marketing avenues/techniques.
- Product/service pricing.
- Export opportunities.
- Infrastructure facilities available.
- Finance and financial institutions.

Similarly, entrepreneurship skill development programmes (ESDPs) are organized to upgrade existing skills and to create new skills in workers and technicians of existing units and educated unemployed youth by organizing various technical training courses for them. The basic objective has been to provide training to unskilled/semi-skilled workers engaged in MSMEs sector and to equip them with better and improved techno-managerial skills of production. Emphasis is given to organize the maximum programmes in rural areas particularly for weaker sections of the society. Specific tailor-made programmes are organized for the skill development of the socially disadvantage groups (OBCs, SCs, STs, minorities and women) in remote regions/pockets of the States. These programmes are also called *Out-Reach Programmes* as these are conducted in rural/less developed areas.

In order to improve the success rate of the entrepreneurship development programme (EDP) trainees in the establishment of new enterprises, the Ministry of MSMEs launched a scheme, namely *Rajiv Gandhi Udyami Mitra Yojana* (a scheme for Promotion and Handholding of Micro and Small Enterprises). The main objective of this scheme is to provide handholding support to first generation entrepreneurs through designated lead agencies, i.e. *Udyami Mitras*.

Under this scheme, the *Udyami Mitras* are providing guidance and assistance to the potential entrepreneurs registered with them in: (a) preparation of project reports, (b) arrangement of finance, (c) selection of technology, (d) marketing tie-ups with buyers, (e) installation of plant and machinery, and (f) obtaining various approvals, clearances etc. For providing this handholding assistance to the new entrepreneurs, the *Udyami Mitras* are paid handholding charges under the scheme, including nominal contribution of the concerned entrepreneur. However, the beneficiaries belonging to SCs, STs, physically handicapped and women are subsidized under the scheme for availing the handholding support from *Udyami Mitra*.

The Indian capacity for harnessing entrepreneurship has not been fully realized. Given the realities of rapidly changing economic landscape in the country, entrepreneurship opportunities have emerged as an important source of meeting the aspirations of the youth. An all inclusive approach to strengthen the entrepreneurship development scenario in the country which is competent, quality conscious, market savvy, innovative and has globally competitive entrepreneurs, needs to be carefully mentored and encouraged.

As the proportion of working age group of 15-59 years will be increasing steadily, India has the advantage of *demographic dividend*. Harnessing the demographic dividend through appropriate skill development efforts would provide an opportunity to achieve inclusion and productivity within the country and also a reduction in the global skill shortages. Large scale skill development is thus an imminent imperative.

Major challenge of skill development initiatives is also to address the needs of huge population by providing skills in order to make them employable and help them secure *decent work.* Skill development for persons working in the unorganized sector is a key strategy in that direction. This will also inculcate dignity of labour and create greater awareness towards environmental, safety and health concerns.

Planned development of skills must be underpinned by a policy which is both comprehensive as well as national in character. A national policy response is, therefore, needed to guide the skill development strategies and coordinated action by all stakeholders to avoid a piecemeal approach. It is also important that the policies of skill development be linked to policies in the economic, employment and social development arenas.

P. Madhavi
G. Satyanarayana

1

Entrepreneurship: An Introduction

The growth and prosperity of all economies remains highly dependent on entrepreneurial activity. Entrepreneurs are the essence of economic growth as they provide a source of income and employment for themselves, create employment for others, produce new and innovative products or services, and drive greater upstream and downstream value-chain activities. Supportive environments are increasingly essential to successful entrepreneurship and these are evolving across the world. The ideal entrepreneurial environment has 5 pillars:

1. Access to funding.
2. Entrepreneurial culture.
3. Supportive regulatory and tax regimes.
4. Educational systems that support entrepreneurial mindsets.
5. A co-ordinated approach that links the public, private and voluntary sectors.

The face of entrepreneurship is also changing. Across the world, entrepreneurs are increasingly young and/or female due to increasing unemployment. The public and private sector each have an important role to play in creating entrepreneurial ecosystems that, in addition to funding, are essential to promoting entrepreneurial success.

Highlighting the diversity of the country, four kinds of entrepreneurial activities exist: (a) factor-driven entrepreneurship, (b) efficiency-driven entrepreneurship, (c) innovation-driven entrepreneurship and (d) necessity-driven entrepreneurship.

Developed economies generate entrepreneurial opportunities as a result of their wealth and innovation capacity, yet they also offer more wage employment options to attract those that might otherwise become independent entrepreneurs. If these opportunities for entrepreneurship and innovation are to be captured, it is essential to create an enabling eco-system for entrepreneurship to thrive and instil a mind-set and culture of opportunity and innovation-based motives and entrepreneurial incentives.

1.1 Who is an Entrepreneur?

An entrepreneur is an individual who organizes and operates a business or businesses, taking on financial risk to do so. The entrepreneur is commonly seen as an innovator of new ideas, and business processes. Management skill and strong team building abilities are often perceived as essential leadership attributes for successful entrepreneurs. Leadership, management ability, and team-building are considered to be the essential qualities of an entrepreneur.

Psychological studies show that the psychological propensities for male and female entrepreneurs are more similar than different. A growing body of work shows that entrepreneurial behaviour is dependent on social and economic factors. For example, countries with healthy and diversified labour markets or stronger safety nets show a more favourable ratio of opportunity-driven rather than necessity-driven women entrepreneurs. Empirical studies suggest that male entrepreneurs possess strong negotiating skills and consensus-forming abilities.

Research studies that explore the characteristics and personality traits of, and influences on, the entrepreneur have come to differing conclusions. Most, however, agree on certain consistent entrepreneurial traits and environmental influences. Although certain entrepreneurial traits are required, entrepreneurial behaviours are also dynamic and influenced by environmental factors. The entrepreneur is solely concerned with opportunity recognition and exploitation, although the opportunity that is recognised depends on the type of entrepreneur.

Some of the most significant influences on an individual's decision to become an entrepreneur are workplace peers and the social composition of the workplace.

The ability of entrepreneurs to innovate is thought to relate to innate traits such as extroversion and a proclivity for risk-taking. The capabilities of innovating, introducing new technologies, increasing efficiency and productivity, or generating new products or services, are characteristic qualities of entrepreneurs. Entrepreneurs are catalysts for economic change, and researchers argue that entrepreneurs are highly creative individuals with a tendency to imagine new solutions by finding opportunities for profit or reward. It is widely maintained that entrepreneurs are unusual individuals. In line with this view, there is an emerging research tradition investigating the genetic factors that are perceived to make entrepreneurs so distinctive.

However, there are also critical perspectives that attribute these research attitudes to oversimplified methodological and/or philosophical assumptions. For example, it has been argued that entrepreneurs are not that distinctive, but that it is in essence unrealistic preconceptions about *non-entrepreneurs* that maintain laudatory portraits of *entrepreneurs*.

1.2 What is Entrepreneurship?

In political economics, entrepreneurship is the quality of being an entrepreneur, i.e. one who *undertakes an enterprise*. The term puts emphasis on the risk and effort taken by individuals who both own and manage a business, and on the innovations resulting from their pursuit of economic success.

Entrepreneurship in this sense may result in new organizations or may be part of revitalizing mature organizations in response to a perceived opportunity. The most obvious form of entrepreneurship is that of starting new businesses (referred as start-up company). In recent years, the term has been extended to include social and political forms of entrepreneurial activity. When entrepreneurship is describing activities within a firm or large organization it is referred to as intra-preneurship and may include corporate venturing, when large entities spin-off organizations.

Entrepreneurial activities are substantially different depending on the type of organization and creativity involved. Entrepreneurship ranges in scale from solo projects (even involving the entrepreneur only part-time) to major undertakings creating many job opportunities. Many high value entrepreneurial ventures seek venture capital or angel funding (seed money) in order to raise capital to build the business. Many kinds of organizations now exist to support would-be entrepreneurs including specialized government agencies, business incubators, science parks, and some NGOs. In more recent times, the term entrepreneurship has been extended to include elements not related necessarily to business formation activity such as conceptualizations of entrepreneurship as a specific mindset resulting in entrepreneurial initiatives e.g. in the form of social entrepreneurship, political entrepreneurship, or knowledge entrepreneurship have emerged.

The supposition that entrepreneurship leads to economic growth is an interpretation of the residual in endogenous growth theory and as such is hotly debated in academic economics. An alternate description suggests that the majority of innovations may be much more incremental improvements such as the replacement of paper with plastic in the construction of a drinking straw.

Entrepreneurship is about taking risk. The behaviour of the entrepreneur reflects a kind of person willing to put his or her career and financial security on the line and take risks in the name of an idea, spending much time as well as capital on an uncertain venture.

The acts of entrepreneurship are often associated with true uncertainty, particularly when it involves bringing something really novel to the world, whose market never exists.

1.3 Role and Importance of Entrepreneurs

Entrepreneurs play an important role in the economic development of a country. Successful entrepreneurs innovate, bring new products and concepts to the market, improve market efficiency, build wealth, create jobs, and enhance economic growth. The ability of entrepreneurs to create jobs is certainly relevant to India, given the need for incremental new jobs.

De novo firms that unleash creative destruction shift surpluses from rent-seeking large producers to consumers and broader society. Joseph Schumpeter, eminent American economist, put innovation at the heart of economic theory and capitalism. He proposed that innovation was the process by which economies were able to break out of their static mode and enter a path of dynamism. It was his theory of *creative destruction* that first highlighted the importance of innovators in revolutionizing the economic structure, leading to the creation of new products, services, and markets, and the decay of the old. Just as boosting entrepreneurship can lead to growth and job creation, failing to promote entrepreneurship can lead to stagnation, and social and economic inertia.

While India celebrates the success of several new ventures in e-commerce, information technology and mobile telephony, these are not sufficient to deliver aggregate growth expectations. The agricultural sector remains moribund, the rural economy neglected, and vast sectors starved of capital and talent, constrained as these are by collective under-investment in the requisite supporting institutions. Similar institutional inadequacy challenges bedevil investments in so-called social enterprises as well. India will have to encourage creation of new small and medium enterprises (SMEs) focused on manufacturing and innovation, while spurring rural innovation and growth. Hence, putting entrepreneurship at the forefront of the economic agenda is the need of the hour.

The ability of entrepreneurs to create jobs is particularly relevant to India given its employment crisis. India's *demographic dividend* [1] must be reaped. By 2020, 63 percent of India's population will be of working age. McKinsey estimates that India's working-age population will grow by 69 million between 2012 and 2022. Cashing in on this dividend will require India to create 69 million additional appropriate jobs, as well as jobs for those that are currently unemployed. Creation of new businesses will therefore be an important avenue for absorption of these workers. Therefore, developing and sustaining a vibrant entrepreneurial fabric is one policy option that should be part and parcel of any economic development plan.

1.4 History of Entrepreneurship in India

India has seen a wave of successful entrepreneurship previously, which started during the time of the Swadeshi Movement. Amongst these entrepreneurs were Jamshedji Tata who founded the Tata Iron and Steel Company (TISCO), P.C. Roy who founded Bengal Chemical Works, V.O. Chidambaran Pillai who founded the Steam Navigation Company, and Khwaja Hamied who founded Cipla, a pharmaceutical company. These firms have played an important role in alleviating the employment crisis over the years.

The entrepreneurial culture in India is picking up. Bangalore has been listed within the world's 20 leading start-up cities in the 2015 Start-up Genome Project ranking. It is also ranked as one of the world's five fastest growing start-up cities. Nevertheless, much of this entrepreneurship is limited to IT.

To create new jobs, India must move beyond its reliance on IT achievements and the industrial conglomerates that drove earlier post-liberalization growth. For example, India needs to develop technological capabilities to serve the requirements of its core industries—capital goods used in manufacturing industries are mostly imported, as are electronic goods.

There is tremendous scope to boost entrepreneurship in India. Some sectors immediately provide opportunities for growth. For example, the auto components sector is expected to see substantial growth as India moves from being the world's seventh largest automobile manufacturer in 2014 to the fourth largest in 2015. Sectors like IT infrastructure, biotechnology, healthcare and education, too are poised to grow several times in size over the next couple of years. There is huge scope in the field of social inclusion.

Bringing the economically disenfranchised (including the dalits, scheduled castes, scheduled tribes, and other backward castes) and women into the economic mainstream not only serves a higher purpose; there is also a strong economic and social justification for the same. It would lead to greater stability in society in the years to come (a benefit across all socio-economic strata), and would also open up a significant new market for firms to tap. As such, it would substantially increase the proportion of the economy that is able to engage in productive activity.

Government policy that favours innovation can have significant impact on growth and job creation in the economy, as indicated by economists that show innovation and productivity to be endogenously generated. Furthermore, India has a latent science and engineering talent pool, which may be particularly advantageous. This strength should be capitalised to generate indigenous intellectual capital.

1.5 Obstacles to Entrepreneurship in India

1. Lack of incentives for innovation at the national level.
2. Lack of efficient business incubators.
3. Insufficient access to capital.
4. Archaic education system.
5. Lack of work-related skills amongst the youth.
6. Disabling business environment.
7. Culture and mindset.

The biggest cultural obstacle to unleashing entrepreneurial potential is middle-class India' scepticism about entrepreneurship. Notwithstanding the exuberance around the IT sector at the moment, in the *mainstream* of the economy, there continues to be suspicion, even distaste, evinced by the idea of entrepreneurship.

Young creative individuals are often held back from starting new ventures due to inherent scepticism amongst family members. Given this cultural context, any blueprint that intends to effectively encourage entrepreneurship must promote and embrace a risk-taking and creative mindset. A related cultural obstacle to innovation is the limited tolerance for failure in Indian society. Experimentation and failure are integral parts of creating and building new ventures. Therefore, a societal tolerance for failure as part and parcel of the learning process needs to be inculcated.

Apart from the overarching theme of a generalized aversion toward risk-taking and failure in India, other more subtle cultural impediments also present a challenge to entrepreneurship and innovation. These include: (a) general sense of apathy and untimeliness in law enforcement, (b) aversion to change within the bureaucracy, (c) culture of rent-seeking at several layers of governance, (d) cultural scepticism toward intellectual property rights and (e) general, pervasive and deeply corrosive sense of mistrust between the government and the private sector.

These factors slow down the private sector in India. Other cultural impediments include a general de-prioritization of soft skills in favour of hard technical knowledge, and a bias by employers against graduates hailing from non-elite institutions or non-engineering backgrounds, amongst others.

To sum up, the Indian capacity for harnessing entrepreneurship has not been fully realized. Given the realities of rapidly changing economic landscape in the country, entrepreneurship opportunities have emerged as an important source of meeting the aspirations of the youth. An all inclusive approach to strengthen the entrepreneurship development scenario in the country which is competent, quality conscious, market savvy, innovative and has globally competitive entrepreneurs, needs to be carefully mentored and encouraged.

Endnote

1. If the massive population of India is properly educated and trained, it can prove a boon for the national economy. India's demographic dividend is essentially due to two factors: (a) declining birth rates and (b) improvement in life expectancy. The declining birth rate changes the age distribution and makes for a smaller proportion of population in the dependent ages and

for relatively larger share in the productive labour force. The result is low dependency ratio which can provide comparative cost advantage and competitiveness to the economy. Moreover, the global economy is expected to witness a skilled man power shortage to the extent of around 56 million by 2020. Thus, the *demographic dividend* in India needs to be exploited not only to expand the production possibility frontier but also to meet the skilled manpower requirements of India and other countries.

2

National Policy for Skill Development and Entrepreneurship (NPSDE), 2015

The Ministry of Labour and Employment, Government of India, had formulated a National Policy on Skill Development in 2009. The objective of this policy was to empower all individuals through improved skills, knowledge, nationally and internationally recognized qualifications to gain access to decent employment and ensure India's competitiveness in the global market.

On July 15, 2015, Prime Minister Shri Narendra Modi launched the National Policy for Skill Development and Entrepreneurship (NPSDE), 2015.

The 2009 policy was, thus, superseded by NPSDE, 2015. The new policy tries to bring the world of education and training closer to the world of work so as to enable them together build a strong India.

The Ministry of Skill Development and Entrepreneurship, Government of India, is an integral part of the government policy on *Sabka Saath, Sabka Vikaas* and its commitment to overall human resources development to take advantage of the demographic profile of India in the coming years. The objective of NPSDE, 2015 is to meet the challenge of skilling at scale with speed and standard (quality). It aims to provide an umbrella framework to all skilling activities being carried out within the country, and to align them to common standards and link the skilling with demand centres. In addition to laying down the objectives and expected outcomes, it also identifies the various institutional frameworks which can act as the vehicle to reach the expected outcomes. The national policy also provides clarity and coherence on how skill development efforts across the country can be aligned within the existing institutional arrangements. This policy links skills development to improved employability and productivity.

The salient features and provisions of NPSDE, 2015 are presented below.

2.1 Vision and Mission

Vision: To create an eco-system of empowerment by skilling on a large scale at speed with high standards and to promote a culture of innovation based entrepreneurship which can generate wealth and employment so as to ensure sustainable livelihoods for all citizens in the country.

Mission: The mission is to:

- Create a demand for skilling across the country.
- Correct and align skilling with required competencies.
- Connect the supply of skilled human resources with sectoral demands.
- Certify and assess in alignment with global and national standards.
- Catalyse an ecosystem wherein productive and innovative entrepreneurship germinates, sustains and grows leading to creation of a more dynamic entrepreneurial economy and more formal wage employment.

2.2 Objectives of NPSDE, 2015

The core objective of NPSDE, 2015, is to empower the individuals by enabling them to realize their full potential through a process of lifelong learning where competencies are accumulated via instruments such as credible certifications, credit accumulation and transfer etc. As individuals grow, the society and nation also benefit from their productivity and growth. This will involve the following:

1. Make quality vocational training aspirational for both youth and employers whereby youth sees it as a matter of choice and employer acknowledges the productivity linked to skilled workforce by paying the requisite premium.
2. Ensure both vertical and horizontal pathways to skilled

workforce for further growth by providing seamless integration of skill training with formal education.

3. Focus on an outcome-based approach towards quality skilling that on the one hand results in increased employability and better livelihoods for individuals, and on the other hand translates into improved productivity across primary, secondary and tertiary sectors.
4. Increase the capacity and quality of training infrastructure and trainers to ensure equitable and easy access to every citizen.
5. Address human resources needs by aligning supply of skilled workers with sectoral requirements of industry and the country's strategic priorities including flagship programmes like Make in India.
6. Establish an IT-based information system for aggregating demand and supply of skilled workforce which can help in matching and connecting supply with demand.
7. Promote national standards in the skilling space through active involvement of employers in setting occupational standards, helping develop curriculum, providing apprenticeship opportunities, participating in assessments, and providing gainful employment to skilled workforce with adequate compensation. Operationalize a well-defined quality assurance framework aligned with global standards to facilitate mobility of labour.
8. Leverage modern technology to ensure scale, access and outreach, in addition to ease of delivering content and monitoring results.
9. Recognise the value of on-the-job training, by making apprenticeships in actual work environments an integral part of all skill development efforts.
10. Ensure that the skilling needs of the socially and geographically disadvantaged and marginalized groups—like the scheduled castes (SCs), scheduled tribes (STs), other backward classes (OBCs), minorities, differently-abled persons—are appropriately taken care of.

11. Promote increased participation of women in the workforce through appropriate skilling and gender mainstreaming of training.
12. Promote commitment and ownership of all stakeholders towards skill development and create an effective coordination mechanism.

The core objective of the entrepreneurship framework is to co-ordinate and strengthen factors essential for growth of entrepreneurship across the country. This would include as under:

1. Promote entrepreneurship culture and make it aspirational.
2. Encourage entrepreneurship as a viable career option through advocacy.
3. Enhance support for potential entrepreneurs through mentorship and networks.
4. Integrate entrepreneurship education in the formal education system.
5. Foster innovation-driven and social entrepreneurship to address the needs of the population at the *bottom of the pyramid.*
6. Ensure ease of doing business by reducing entry and exit barriers.
7. Facilitate access to finance through credit and market linkages.
8. Promote entrepreneurship amongst women.
9. Broaden the base of entrepreneurial supply by meeting specific needs of both socially and geographically disadvantaged sections of the society including SCs, STs, OBCs, minorities, differently-abled persons.

2.3 Policy Framework for Skill Development: Eleven-point Strategy

The policy framework has been developed to accomplish the vision of 'Skill India' by adhering to the objectives mentioned above. The framework outlines the following 11 major paradigms and enablers to achieve these objectives of skilling India:

1. **Aspiration and Advocacy:** The need of the hour is to

make skill development aspirational for boys and girls. For skill training to be looked at as a matter of choice, it must: (a) provide vertical growth pathways on the lines of the general education system, so that skill education and training is also seen as a valid route to earn degrees and diplomas, and consequently to positions of authority linked to such qualifications, (b) be associated with growth and sustainable livelihood pathways and (c) have a causal relationship with increased income for skilled workforce.

2. **Capacity:** The annual skilling in the country was estimated at around 7 million in 2014. In the current landscape, capacity is being created by private sector training organisations, industry in-house training, government and private industrial training institutes (ITIs), advanced training institutes (ATIs), tool rooms and in schools, colleges and polytechnics. For all existing and new capacity that will be generated, the focus will move from inputs to outcomes of skill training that include employability and placements of trainees. Incentives will be linked to placement in all training institutions. For Government supported schemes, funding will be linked to outcomes of the training programmes.
3. **Quality:** One-Nation-One-Standard should become the *mantra* to ensure that national standards and quality for skilling are globally aligned and Indian youth can aspire to secure local, national and international job opportunities. Quality of training can be measured by competency outcomes and employability of trainees. The following parameters have been identified for improving quality:

- Quality assurance framework embedded in NSQF. [1]
- Market relevant training programmes.
- Recognition of prior learning.
- Curriculum alignment.
- National certification framework.
- Employability skills.
- Placements.

4. **Synergy:** Skill development programmes being implemented by various Ministries, Departments and Agencies of the Central Government have different norms as regards the eligibility criteria, duration of training, maximum amount for training, outcomes, monitoring and tracking mechanism etc. This multiplicity of norms and parameters results in avoidable difficulties in implementation and makes it difficult to evaluate the performance of the skill development programmes across the Central Government in an objective manner.
5. **Mobilization and Engagement:** Industry needs to be closely involved in providing job opportunities to the skilled workforce. Industry will be encouraged to increasingly move towards employing only certified skilled people. In addition, employers need to rationalize the compensation paid across different levels of skills to award a skill premium for increased productivity as a result of higher skills.
6. **Global Partnerships:** The main objective of global partnerships and international collaborations is to leverage best practices from across the world. Such collaborations will immensely enrich domestic training programmes by enhancing their quality through learnings from successful international models of vocationalization of education, engaging with industry etc. Institutional arrangements through joint working groups, secretariats etc will be established for regular exchange of knowledge, experiences, research findings, teaching and learning materials, and innovations in skill development.
7. **Outreach:** The proposed KVKs will play a pivotal role in identifying local employment opportunities and providing adequate training and post-training support according to needs of local areas such as migration support for skilled workers. The centres will also function as information centres for training and employment opportunities, as well as for various support schemes. KVKs in the form of

mobile training facilities, will also be deployed to reach out to remote and difficult areas.

8. **ICT Enablement:** Promotion of only brick and mortar facilities will not ensure the speed and scale desired to transform the skill development efforts. The use of technology will be leveraged to scale up training facilities, enable access to remote areas and increase cost-effectiveness of delivery of vocational training. Government will also look to support innovative products, solutions and models that address critical gaps in skill ecosystem in an effective manner. Use of existing available networks such as the widespread optical fibre network will be optimized.
9. **Trainers and Assessors:** To achieve the massive target of skilling, it is of utmost importance to have quality trainers who are capable of training people in several fields. Similarly, quality assessors in sufficient numbers are also required to ensure consistent outcomes of assessment and certification process. Government will decisively intervene, directly or through other stakeholders, to bring more experienced people in training and assessment space, especially ex-servicemen in defence and retired/working people from industry.
10. **Inclusivity:** It is necessary to promote skill development initiatives that will ensure inclusivity, irrespective of gender, location, caste, sector etc. One of the key objectives is to safeguard the skilling needs of SCs, STs, OBCs, minorities, and differently-abled persons, as well as those living in difficult geographical pockets.
11. **Promotion of Skilling amongst Women:** According to Census Data 2011, women account for 48.5 percent of the entire population in India. Women have the capability to further drive the economy of the country if their participation in the workforce is increased. With the help of skilling, women can have viable incomes, decent work and be major players who can contribute equally to the economic growth of the country.

2.4 Policy Framework for Entrepreneurship: Nine-point Strategy

The entrepreneurship policy framework has been developed to address the objectives. Vibrant entrepreneurship requires support from an enabling eco-system of culture, finance, expertise, infrastructure, skills and business-friendly regulations. Many government and non-government organizations are playing enabling roles across each of these crucial supporting elements. This policy framework, cognizant of the need for the full eco-system to be present to unlock entrepreneurial potential, proposes the following nine part entrepreneurship strategy:

1. **Educate and Equip Potential and Early Stage Entrepreneurs Across India:** In partnership with experts, a world class entrepreneurship education curriculum will be developed. Through a blend of online and experiential learning, potential entrepreneurs will go through hands-on, student-centric courses that help them acquire skills they need to start an enterprise. This curriculum will build on and adapt the best entrepreneurship education content available globally.
2. **Connect Entrepreneurs to Peers, Mentors and Incubators:** To support young entrepreneurs, a web and mobile-based platform connecting the entire entrepreneurial ecosystem will be established. Students, young entrepreneurs, mentors, incubators, funding agencies and basic service providers will all be able to log in and connect to each other in their respective industries and locations.
3. **Support Entrepreneurs through Entrepreneurship Hubs (E-Hubs):** Support to entrepreneurs, including coordinated delivery of national and state government entrepreneurship programmes and access to enabling resources, a national network of entrepreneurship hubs (e-hubs) will be established.
4. **Catalyse a Culture Shift to Encourage Entrepreneurship:** To promote entrepreneurship, state and national level interaction with stakeholders will be convened. Keynote

speakers from industry, both domestic and international, will be invited to share best practice from the field. International linkages will also be established through internship opportunities and exchange trips to global entrepreneurship hubs such as Silicon Valley and Israel.

5. **Encourage Entrepreneurship among Under-represented Groups:** Special focus will be given to the inclusion of scheduled castes and scheduled tribes, minorities, differently-abled, etc. and regionally under-represented areas including large part of Eastern and North-Eastern India in entrepreneurship programmes.
6. **Promote Entrepreneurship amongst Women:** The Economic Survey conducted for India by OECD in November 2014 clearly enlists low female economic participation as one of the major findings. Creating more and better employment for women has high growth potential. Currently, the contribution of women in workforce is limited to only 24 percent. Head of UN Women has also indicated that India's GDP will leapfrog by another 4.2 percent if women in India can contribute their full potential to the economy.
7. **Improve Ease of Doing Business:** A business-friendly environment with easy entry and exit procedures will encourage entrepreneurial activity. The following actions to rationalise business procedures and regulations through the following initiatives should be investigated:

- Introduce unique enterprise number (UEN) that a new enterprise could use for various registrations including taxes, labour laws and social security. Once UEN is available, all regulatory and support agencies shall use it to fasten the process of setting up an enterprise.
- Introduce an online composite application form (CAF) that will help entrepreneurs file a single application for obtaining all approvals and clearances from various government authorities.
- Encourage states to strengthen existing single window

system with a high power committee empowered to give all necessary clearances for setting up a business.

- Convert the present district industries centres (DICs) into business development centres (BDCs) with an objective to provide technical and procedural hand-holding support and counselling to pre-start-up, nascent, early start-up and growth ventures.
- Permit flexibility to start-ups in hiring and retaining workforce for operational adjustments and rationalisation during the first 3 years of operation of an enterprise, assuming that by the end of 3 years it will either stabilise and grow or become sick and close down.
- Allow easy exit to enterprises if they have been in operation for less than 3 years. Such enterprises will be facilitated to close their operations, if not found viable, within a period of 3 months. Special fast track court would be set up to expedite the process of closure of such firms.
- Consider tax incentives to new and existing entrepreneurs.

8. **Improve Access to Finance:** As per RBI data, the share of small-scale industries in gross bank credit from scheduled commercial banks has been continuously decreasing. Its share has fallen from 15.42 percent of the gross bank credit in 1991 to 6.34 percent in 2006-07. To reinvigorate the flow of credit to deserving entrepreneurs, the following interventions could be considered:

- Ensure that credit delivery norms are met by financial institutions without compromising the quality of the projects submitted for credit.
- Strengthen venture capital companies in quasi-public sector by infusing capital through equity participation.
- Incentivise Angel financing by providing appropriate rebates on capital gains made by investors.
- Promote a *rescue* culture by revisiting bankruptcy rules and facilitate counselling and advisory services to troubled firms by appropriately addressing legal status.
- Encourage national and state bodies, viz. National

Scheduled Caste Finance and Development Corporation (NSCFDC), National Minorities Development and Finance Corporation (NMDFC), National Backward Classes Finance and Development Corporation (NBCFDC), to provide credit to micro enterprise start-ups launched by their target population.

- Explore the possibility of setting up a national fund for the unorganised sector, as recommended by the National Commission for Enterprises in the Unorganised Sector in 2007, to hasten the process of achieving inclusive growth of entrepreneurship.
- Encourage and support financial institutions to develop innovative micro level financial tools to enhance investibility in micro ventures. Further, they would also be encouraged to increase lending in rural areas through self-help groups and innovative micro financing.

9. **Foster Social Entrepreneurship and Grassroots Innovations:** Social enterprises have emerged as important business instruments to address the issues of poverty, unemployment and inequity in society, through socially-oriented business innovations. Social innovation seeks to answer these social problems by offering new products and services which allow the poor to interact with markets as active participants rather than passive recipients. Considering the need to encourage such social enterprises, the following will be undertaken:

- Encourage universities and academic institutions to launch a course on social entrepreneurship, including online distance education, to actively promote social entrepreneurship in the country.
- Foster a social capital market place by offering fiscal incentives to attract investors and make provision for funding support under a separate scheme(s) like social venture fund, to facilitate social entrepreneurs' access to credit.
- Facilitate creation of social enterprises even with a modest capital base, through social incubates across the country.

- Encourage innovators, universities and institutions to patent innovative entrepreneurship ideas and technologies by promoting and strengthening intellectual property rights (IPRs).
- Create grassroots technology innovation hubs to harness the innovation potential of grassroots innovators.
- Promote and encourage grassroots innovations and assist innovators to commercialise and up-scale their products and services.
- To encourage innovation, collaborate with organisations such as the National Innovation Foundation to encourage grassroots technological innovation and integrate with the national research and innovation ecosystem. Using the national network of e-hubs and other platforms, assist entrepreneurs in commercializing and scaling up their products and services.

2.5 Governance Structure and Financing

2.5.1 Governance Structure: Ministry of Skill Development and Entrepreneurship has been created to fulfil the vision of a Skilled India where human resources development is the primary focus. MSDE will be responsible for co-ordination with all concerned for evolving an appropriate skill development framework, removal of disconnect between demand for, and supply of, skilled manpower, skill upgradation, building of new skills, innovative thinking and talents for existing and future jobs. MSDE will also play the lead role in ensuring the implementation of the National Policy for Skill Development and Entrepreneurship, 2015.

Skill development and entrepreneurship are complementary to each other. The key stakeholders include Central Ministries, State Governments, and industry/employers. There is a need to ensure alignment of the efforts of all stakeholders in skill and entrepreneurship landscape towards a common goal. While MSDE will co-ordinate and converge all efforts in this space, the relevant Central Ministries/Departments, State Governments and industry/employers are expected to fulfil the roles and responsibilities pertaining to their domain as laid down in the National Policy for Skill Development and Entrepreneurship.

The objectives and targets under the National Policy will be met in mission mode approach. The National Skill Development Mission will be launched to implement and co-ordinate all skilling efforts in the country towards the objectives laid down in the policy. The Mission will be housed in MSDE and the key institutional mechanisms for achieving the objectives of the Mission will be divided into a three-tier structure at the Centre to steer, drive and execute the Mission's objectives. The Mission will consist of a governing council at apex level, a steering committee and a mission directorate (along with an Executive Committee) as the executive arm of the Mission. At State level, States will be encouraged to create State Skill Development Missions (SSDM) along the lines of National Skill Development Mission with a steering committee and mission directorate at State level. States will, in turn, be supported by district committees at the functional tier.

Mission directorate will be supported by three other institutions: National Skill Development Agency (NSDA), National Skill Development Corporation (NSDC), and Directorate General of Training (DGT) all of which will have horizontal/vertical linkages with Mission Directorate to facilitate smooth functioning of the national institutional mechanism.

2.5.2 National Skill Development Agency (NSDA): NSDA was set up as a Society in June 2013. NSDA will focus on the two verticals of quality assurance and policy research in the skills space. It will be chiefly responsible for the following activities:

1. Operationalise and implement National Skills Qualification Framework (NSQF).
2. Establish and operationalise a QA framework embedded in NSQF to improve consistency of outcomes in the skills landscape, which will include laying down a framework

for training, assessment and certification processes and agencies in the country.

3. Operationalise National Skills Qualification Committee (NSQC) to meet its objectives.
4. Design and implement the National Labour Market Information System.
5. Develop national protocols for registration and accreditation of private training providers.
6. Promote use of Skill India logo on skill certificates by SSCs/agencies adhering to the QA framework.
7. Anchor Prime Minister's Skill Development Fellow Programme.

National Skills Research Division (NSRD), under NSDA will be established to serve as the apex division for providing technical and research support to the Mission. This division will act as a think-tank for MSDE and be the core skill development hub, which will connect implementation of the Mission with academic research and data. Its 4 key functions will include research, policy advisory/inputs, career support and knowledge exchange networks.

2.5.3 National Skill Development Corporation (NSDC): NSDC, a public private partnership was set up in 2008 as a Section 25 company under Companies Act, 1956 with shareholding of Government of India at 49 percent and that of the private sector at 51 percent. It will be the nodal organization for all private sector initiatives in the short-term skilling space. Its mandate will primarily include the following:

1. Catalyse the creation of market-based, scalable business by providing funding through a combination of debt, equity and grants.
2. Implementing skills voucher programme.
3. Driving engagement with industry and businesses.
4. Promote centres of excellence for training of trainers in coordination with States and SSCs.
5. Initiating and incubating sector skills councils (SSCs).

6. Discharge any other function as may be assigned to it by the Ministry.

2.5.4 Directorate General of Training: The two verticals of training and apprenticeship training under DGET, MoLE have been shifted to MSDE from April 16, 2015. Its large institutional framework consisting of ITIs, ATIs, RVTIs and other national institutes will act as tools of execution for Mission activities. Other functions will include the following:

1. Setting up framework for structure of courses, assessment, curricula creation, affiliation and accreditation of institutes, under NCVT.
2. Develop national standards on syllabi, equipment, scale of space, duration of courses and methods of training.
3. Advise on training policy in its network of training institutes.
4. Co-ordinate functioning of industrial training institutes (ITIs).
5. Run training programmes for training of trainers and instructors.
6. Run special institutes for training of women.
7. Leverage field infrastructure for strong industry interface in all facets of training, including on-the-job training.
8. Provide technical support to vocational education across the country.
9. Anchor and operationalise Apprentices Act, 1961 as overhauled by comprehensive amendments in December 2014.
10. Operationalise various training schemes through ITIs and vocational training providers (VTPs).

2.5.5 Sector Skill Councils (SSCs): In order to ensure that skill development efforts being made by all stakeholders in the system are in accordance with actual needs of industry, SSCs are being set up. SSCs are industry-led and industry-governed bodies, which will help link the requirements of industry with appropriately trained manpower.

SSCs will discharge the following functions:

1. Identification of skill development needs including preparing a catalogue of types of skills, range and depth of skills to facilitate individuals to choose from them.
2. Development of a sector skill development plan and maintenance of skill inventory.
3. Determining skills, competency standards and qualifications and getting them notified as per NSQF.
4. Standardization of affiliation, accreditation, examination and certification process in accordance with NSQF as determined by NSQC. May also conduct skill-based assessment and certification for QP/NOS-aligned training programmes.
5. Participation in the setting up of affiliation, accreditation, examination and certification norms for their respective sectors.
6. Plan and facilitate the execution of training of trainers along with NSDC and States.
7. Promotion of academies of excellence.
8. Lay special emphasis on the skilling needs of STs/SCs, differently-abled and minority populations.
9. SSCs shall ensure that the persons trained and skilled in accordance with the norms laid down by them are assured of employment at decent wages.

2.5.6 Entrepreneurship Institutes: National Institute for Entrepreneurship and Small Business Development (NIESBUD) and Indian Institute of Entrepreneurship (IIE), Guwahati were transferred to MSDE on May 2, 2015. NIEBUD is a society engaged in training, consultancy, research and publication, in order to promote entrepreneurship. It is operating from an integrated campus in NOIDA, Uttar Pradesh, and its major activities include training, conducting research/evaluation studies, developing course curricula/syllabi for entrepreneurship development programmes, undertaking development programmes in clusters, running an incubation centre etc. IIE's objectives include promotion and development of entrepreneurship, conducting research, providing consultancy for entrepreneurship development, providing consultancy and monitoring service to MSMEs/potential entrepreneurs and enhancing employability of participants. Further, a national advisory committee comprising of representatives/members from all relevant Ministries, industry, academia, specialized institutions, funding agencies and young entrepreneurs engaged in promoting entrepreneurship etc. will be set up to institutionalise entrepreneurship development in the country.

2.5.7 Financing: Public funds (funding by Central Government, State Governments and grant-based schemes) are finite and will not be able to cover the magnitude of the challenge of Skilling India. Hence, alternative sources of funds are required. Therefore, all stakeholders, the Government, both at Centre and States, public and private enterprises, and the direct beneficiary (the individual), would contribute in mobilizing financial or in-kind resources for skill development. The success of the policy will depend upon the quantum of resources mobilised from all stakeholders.

National Skill Development Fund (NSDF) has been set up by Government of India with the objective of encouraging skill development in the country. A Public Trust set up by Government of India is the custodian of the Fund. The Fund acts as a receptacle for all donations, contribution in cash or kind from all contributors (including Government, multilateral organizations, corporations etc.) for furtherance of the objectives of the Fund.

To channelize the interest of a plethora of organisations to participate in the mission of Skill India, a strategic vehicle to create a multiplier effect on skilling has been devised. A 'Resource Optimization for Skilling at Scale Platform' has been proposed by the Government to act as a demand-responsive and flexible vehicle to tackle the issues of skills shortages through skill development, job creation and placement at scale. It will serve as the aggregator vehicle for pooling the funds of multilateral agencies, companies, foundations, NGOs and individuals for skilling interventions by leveraging existing infrastructure and resources. The platform will also be subjected to timely audits to ensure that the contributions are used for the intended purpose.

To attract funds from industry, companies will be encouraged to spend at least 25 percent of their corporate social responsibility (CSR) funds on skill development initiatives directly or through NSDF. Further, industry should earmark at least 2 percent of its payroll bill (including for contract labour) for skill development initiatives in their respective sectors. These funds can be channelized for skill development activities either through respective SSCs or through NSDF.

All Government schemes across sectors will be encouraged to apportion a certain percentage (10 percent) of the scheme budget towards skilling of human resources in local regions in the required sector. These funds could be used for implementation directly or be routed through NSDF. Government may consider other options including cess etc. to raise funds for meeting the requirements of this sector.

End-user funding through a basic fee paying model will also be a key medium for funding training activities. However, the Government believes that the inability to pay training costs should not stop any desirous citizen in the country from acquiring any certified skill training. The Government will promote grant of scholarships, rewards and skill vouchers (SV) for funding of training costs. It will also be ensured that for all government schemes, direct benefit transfer (DBT) will be used as a mechanism for payment disbursement.

A Credit Guarantee Fund for skill development and a National Credit Guarantee Trustee Company (NCGTC) has been set up to support the initiative of loans for the purpose of skilling and will be used to leverage credit financing in the skill landscape. It will be further expanded to ensure greater outreach and access to all citizens. Similarly, a Credit Guarantee Fund for Entrepreneurship Development worth ₹ 3,000 crore per year has already been initiated under Prime Minister MUDRA Yojna through NCGTC.

2.6 Monitoring and Evaluation

The National Policy for Skill Development and Entrepreneurship has been structured as an outcome-oriented policy. It is, therefore, desirable that there should be regular monitoring and evaluation of the initiatives to ensure that best practices can be scaled and corrective measures can be introduced. The main idea of having a robust monitoring and evaluation mechanism is to ensure successful implementation of the policy initiatives.

Government desires to set up a policy implementation unit (PIU) so as to review the implementation and progress of the various initiatives under this policy. The PIU will be housed in MSDE with Secretary as the Chairperson and representation from NITI Aayog. For the smooth functioning of the PIU, it will also ensure constant consultation with stakeholders to get feedback so as to enable improvements, if required.

The PIU will perform the following functions:

1. List all the action points as mentioned in the policy on which further action is required.
2. Identify all the agencies involved and map the actionable points to the responsible agency.
3. Co-ordinate with all the agencies involved and help them devise a draft outline as well as timelines for the implementation of the initiatives assigned to them.
4. Timelines that are explicitly mentioned in the policy for certain initiatives will supersede other timelines.
5. Act as a co-ordinating body for all the implementing agencies and support them to enhance their efficiency.
6. PIU will also conduct monthly review of the action points and nudge them if the progress is not as expected.

PIU will be made responsible to the NSDM. It will present its reports, findings and the way forward to the Steering Committee of the Mission every quarter. PIU will be the main body overlooking the implementation of policy.

2.6.1 Impact Assessment: For the purpose of undertaking impact assessment, annual as well as 5 year targets will be set for each stakeholder by the PIU. Impact assessment will be undertaken to ensure that the targets are met well within the time frame. The stakeholders will also be subject to a quarterly review. For the purpose of impact assessment, the following monitoring indicators, amongst others, are prescribed:

1. Number/registrations of youth interested in skilling.
2. Number of youth registered in training programmes.
3. Number of youth assessed and certified by regulatory authorities.
4. Placement rate of skilled trainees.
5. Number of accredited/affiliated training providers/centres.
6. Number of certified trainers, sector-wise.
7. Number of certified assessors, sector-wise.
8. Number of job roles for which QPs and NOS have been developed.
9. Existing public infrastructure leveraged for training.
10. Number of skilled persons engaged in overseas employment.
11. Reduction in sectoral demand and supply gap.
12. Amount of private funds mobilised for encouraging skill development and entrepreneurship.
13. Percentage of socially and geographically disadvantaged groups enrolled in training programmes.
14. Percentage of skilled youth that are self-employed.
15. Infrastructure dedicated for entrepreneurship support.
16. Number of schools running skills and entrepreneurship courses.
17. Percentage of socially and geographically disadvantaged groups engaged in self employment.

With the help of the PIU, it will be easier to monitor the implementation of the policy initiatives and take corrective measures in case of non-compliance. A mid-term review of the policy will be undertaken based on impact assessment by a third party. The policy can be considered for review after 5 years, based on learnings from implementation of the policy.

To sum up, NPSDE, 2015 has four thrust areas. It

addresses key obstacles to skilling, including low aspirational value, lack of integration with formal education, lack of focus on outcomes, low quality of training infrastructure and trainers etc. Further, it seeks to align supply and demand for skills by bridging existing skill gaps, promoting industry engagement, operationalising a quality assurance framework, leverage technology and promoting greater opportunities for apprenticeship training.

Equity is also a focus of NPSDE, 2015, which targets skilling opportunities for socially and geographically marginalised and disadvantaged groups. Skill development and entrepreneurship programmes for women are a specific focus area. In the entrepreneurship domain, it seeks to educate and equip potential entrepreneurs, both within and outside the formal education system. It also seeks to connect entrepreneurs to mentors, incubators and credit markets, foster innovation and entrepreneurial culture, improve ease of doing business and promote a focus on social entrepreneurship.

The primary objective of NPSDE, 2015 is to meet the challenge of skilling at scale with speed, standard (quality) and sustainability. It aims to provide an umbrella framework to all skilling activities being carried out within the country, to align them to common standards and link skilling with demand centres. In addition to laying down the objectives and expected outcomes, it also identifies the overall institutional framework which will act as a vehicle to reach the expected outcomes. Skills development is the shared responsibility of the key stakeholders, viz. Government, the entire spectrum of corporate sector, community-based organizations, highly qualified and dedicated individuals, industry and trade organisations and other stakeholders.

NPSDE, 2015 links skills development to improved employability and productivity in paving the way forward for inclusive growth in the country. The skill strategy is complemented by specific efforts to promote entrepreneurship in order to create ample opportunities for the skilled workforce.

Endnote

1. National Skills Qualification Framework (NSQF) is an important institutional mechanism that ensures consistency of nationally recognized qualifications both for formal and non-formal skills-based education and training. It accommodates experiential life-long learning through mechanisms such as recognition of prior learning, improves the alignment of formal and non-formal training programmes with industry requirements; and increases options for students by broadening programme and progression for learners through horizontal and vertical pathways.

3

Entrepreneurship Development Institutes in India

3.1 National Level Entrepreneurship Development Institutes

Entrepreneurship has been considered the backbone of economic development. It has been well-established that the level of economic growth of a region, to a large extent, depends on the level of entrepreneurial activities in the region. The myth that entrepreneurs are born, no more holds good. Rather, it is well-recognised now that the entrepreneurs can be created and nurtured through appropriate interventions in the form of entrepreneurship development programmes.

In the era of liberalisation, privatisation and globalization along with ongoing IT revolution, capable entrepreneurs are making use of the opportunities emerging from the evolving scenario. However, a large segment of the population, particularly in the industrially backward regions/rural areas generally lags behind in taking advantage of these opportunities. Therefore, there is a need to provide skill development and entrepreneurship development training to such people in order to bring them to mainstream of economic growth.

Entrepreneurship development programmes (EDPs) are being organized as a regular training activity to cultivate the latent qualities of youth by enlightening them on various aspects that are necessary to be considered while setting up enterprises. These programmes are conducted generally for technicians/artisans for motivating them towards self-employment. The course contents of such EDPs are so designed as to provide useful information on: (a) product/process design, (b) manufacturing practices involved, (c) testing and quality control, (d) selection and usage of appropriate machinery and equipments, (e) project profile preparation, (f) marketing avenues/techniques, (g) product/service pricing, (h) export opportunities, (i) infrastructure facilities available, (j) finance and financial institutions, and (k) cash flows. No fees are charged from scheduled castes, scheduled tribes, women and physically handicapped participants in the stipendiary programmes. Rather they are eligible for a stipend of ₹ 125 per week. Emphasis is given to special programmes in rural areas particularly for weaker sections of the society.

Similarly, entrepreneurship skill development programmes (ESDPs) are organized to upgrade existing skills and to create new skills in workers and technicians of existing units and educated unemployed youth by organizing various technical training courses for them. The basic objective has been to provide training to unskilled/semi-skilled workers engaged in MSMEs sector and to equip them with better and improved techno-managerial skills of production. Emphasis is given to organize the maximum programmes in rural areas particularly for weaker sections of the society. Specific tailor-made programmes are organized for the skill development of the socially disadvantage groups (OBCs, SCs, STs, minorities and women) in remote regions/pockets of the States. These programmes are also called *Out-Reach Programmes* as these are conducted in rural/less developed areas.

Entrepreneurship development and training is, thus, one of the key elements for development of MSMEs, particularly the first generation entrepreneurs. To undertake this task on regular basis, the Ministry of MSMEs has set up the following 3 national-level entrepreneurship development institutes (EDIs) as autonomous bodies. These institutes are engaged in: (a) developing training modules, (b) undertaking research and training and (c) providing consultancy services for entrepreneurship development and promotion of MSMEs, including enhancement of their competitiveness.

1. National Institute for Micro, Small and Medium Enterprises (NI-MSME), Hyderabad.
2. National Institute for Entrepreneurship and Small Business

Development (NIESBUD), NOIDA (Uttar Pradesh).
3. Indian Institute of Entrepreneurship (IIE), Guwahati.

3.1.1 National Institute for Micro, Small and Medium Enterprises (NIMSME), Hyderabad: It is an organization of the Ministry of MSMEs, Government of India. NI-MSME was originally set up as Central Industrial Extension Training Institute (CIETI) in New Delhi in 1960 as a Department under the Ministry of Industry and Commerce, Government of India. It was decided to keep it free from the tardy and impeding administrative controls and procedures, so that the Institute can play a pivotal role in the promotion of small enterprise. Therefore, the Institute was shifted to Hyderabad in 1962, and was renamed as Small Industry Extension Training (SIET) Institute.

A. Centres of Excellence: SIET was conferred the status of national institute by the Government of India with the charter of assisting in the promotion of small enterprises mainly by creating a pro-business environment. In 1984, UNIDO recognised SIET as an institute of meritorious performance under its Centres of Excellence Scheme. Subsequently, it was also accorded the national status in the same year and SIET Institute became NI-SIET. Since then, the Institute has come a long way, carving a place of distinction for itself in the domain of entrepreneurship promotion, achieving recognition both at the national level and in the international arena. To cope with the pressure of globalisation, the Government of India enacted the MSMED Act which became effective from 2nd October 2006. Accordingly, the Institute, in order to reflect the expanded focus of its objectives with name was rechristened as NI-MSME from April 11, 2007 and re-designed its structure and organisation. It is an organisation of the Ministry of Micro, Small and Medium Enterprises.

3.1.2 National Institute for Entrepreneurship and Small Business Development (NIESBUD), NOIDA, (Uttar Pradesh): NIESBUD [1] is a premier institute established in 1983 for coordinating and over viewing the activities of various institutions/agencies engaged in developing entrepreneurship, primarily in small industry, small business and human resources development. NIESBUD has been actively engaged in organizing national/international training programmes, which have benefited MSMEs in India and in other countries.

A. Objectives of NIESBUD: These are as follows:

1. To evolve standardised materials and processes for selection, training, support and sustenance of entrepreneurs, potential and existing.
2. To help/support and affiliate institutions/organisations in carrying out training and other entrepreneurship development related activities.
3. To serve as an apex national level resource institute for accelerating the process of entrepreneurship development ensuring its impact across the country and among all strata of the society.
4. To provide vital information and support to trainers, promoters and entrepreneurs by organising research and documentation activities relevant to entrepreneurship development.
5. To train trainers, promoters and consultants in various areas of entrepreneurship development.
6. To offer consultancy nationally/internationally for promotion of entrepreneurship and small business development.
7. To provide national/international forums for interaction and exchange of experiences helpful for policy formulation and modification at various levels.
8. To share international experience and expertise in entrepreneurship development.
9. To share experience and expertise in entrepreneurship development across national frontiers.

B. Activities of NIESBUD:

(a) Assisting/Supporting EDPs:

- Evolving standardized materials, research, and publications.
- Formulation of standardised procedures of identification and

selection of potential entrepreneurs.

- Preparation of training aids materials: (a) manuals, (b) handbooks, (c) lesson plans, (d) learning text, (e) case studies, and (f) EMT kits etc.

(b) Training of Trainers/Promoters:

- Accreditation programme for entrepreneurial motivation trainers.
- Trainers' training programme for enterprise launching and management.
- Trainers/promoters programme for support organizations.
- Small business promotion programme.
- Entrepreneurship orientation programme for senior executives.

(c) Research and Publications:

- Research on topics related to entrepreneurship and allied areas: (a) disseminates the findings widely, (b) status analysis study on entrepreneurship in India, (c) potential of women entrepreneurship in India, (d) successful women entrepreneurs, their identity, expectations and problems and (e) directory of EDP institutions in India.
- Information materials for entrepreneurs like handbooks on industrial laws, commercial laws, ready reckoner for product selection etc.
- Directory of experts.
- Newsletter covering schemes, news, views, forthcoming activities, agency profile, entrepreneurial profile etc.

(d) Creation and Capacity Building of EDP Institutions:

The Institute provides support and guidance in establishing EDP institutions. The assistance covers developing programmes and faculty, providing training, library facilities and sharing experiences of conducting programmes at the initial stage(s).

(e) Small Business in Focus: The Institute focuses its attention on small business development by encouraging and supporting arrangements in remote and backward areas. The number and percentage of small business among small entrepreneurs is very large. The Institute concentrates its efforts on evolving methodology for training, supporting and sustaining this Group.

(f) National/International Forum for Exchange of Ideas and Experiences

- The Institute organises national as well as international meets for sharing experiences with a view to enhance success in implementation of entrepreneurship development programmes.
- Organises workshops and seminars on contemporary topics/issues such as sustaining entrepreneurship, emerging entrepreneurial opportunities etc.
- Encourages foreign delegations for mutual exchange of experiences.

(g) Developing Entrepreneurial Culture:

- The Institute strives to create climate conducive to emergence of entrepreneurs from all strata of society.
- Conducts awareness campaigns for students of school and college and institutions of higher learnings.
- Produces and distributes material for use by mass media like television etc.
- Organises group discussions representing a variety of cross-section of the society.

(h) Services to Affiliate Members: The Institute affiliates individuals, institutions and organisations engaged in entrepreneurship development and related activities such as ordinary, associate and corporate members. The Institute offers the following services to the members:

- Discussing strategy for propagating entrepreneurship.
- Provision of concessional facilities.
- Free services (library, documentation etc.).
- Free academic advice/guidance.

(i) Sustaining Entrepreneurship: Sustaining existing entrepreneurs is an important activity. In this direction, the Institute organises continuing education programmes for small entrepreneurs besides providing counselling and consultancy. Short duration training programmes on working capital management, marketing, project identification and selection, accounting etc. are conducted on campus while counselling is provided on and off the campus.

3.1.3 Indian Institute of Entrepreneurship (IIE), Guwahati [2]: With an aim to undertake training, research and consultancy activities in small and micro enterprises focusing on entrepreneurship development, IIE was established in the year 1993 in Guwahati by the erstwhile Ministry of Industry (now the Ministry of Micro, Small and Medium Enterprises), Government of India as an autonomous national institute. The Institute began operating from April 1994 with the North East Council (NEC), Governments of Assam, Arunachal Pradesh and Nagaland and SIDBI as its other stakeholders.

A. Objectives: Following are the objectives of IIE:

1. To organize and conduct training for entrepreneurship development.
2. To evolve strategies and methodologies for different target groups and locations and conduct field tests.
3. To identify training needs and offer training programmers to Government and non-Government organizations engaged in promoting and supporting entrepreneurship.
4. To document and disseminate information needed for policy formulation and implementation related to self-employment.
5. To identify, design and conduct training programmers for existing entrepreneurs.
6. To prepare and publish literature related to entrepreneurship and industrial development.
7. To organize seminars, workshops and confer conferences for providing a forum for interaction and exchange of views by various agencies and entrepreneurs.
8. To conduct research for generating knowledge to accelerate the process of entrepreneurship development.
9. To act as a catalyst for development of self-employment, entrepreneurship, industry/business.
10. To evolve, design and help in the utilization of various media for creating entrepreneurship.

B. Activities: The activities of IIE include the following:

1. Identification of training needs.
2. Designing and organizing programmes, both for development functionaries and entrepreneurs.
3. Evolving effective training strategies and methodologies for different target groups and locations.
4. Organizing seminars, workshops and conferences for providing fora for interaction and exchange of views by various agencies and entrepreneurs.
5. Undertaking research on entrepreneurship development.
6. Documenting and disseminating information needed for policy formulation and implementation on self-employment and entrepreneurship.

IIE acts as a catalyst for entrepreneurship development by creating an environment for entrepreneurship in the support system, developing new entrepreneurship, helping in the growth of existing entrepreneurs and propagation of entrepreneurial education.

Considering the importance of creating environment for entrepreneurship development, IIE has been organizing a number of programmes to create awareness about entrepreneurship. Creating awareness on entrepreneurship among the students has been one of the core areas of IIE. It organizes faculty development programmes for university and college teachers and awareness camps for students of colleges.

In keeping with the trend of the recent worldwide phenomenon of entrepreneurship development through area approach, IIE initiated cluster development efforts to develop the languishing small and traditional industrial sector in the North Eastern Region with financial linkage.

IIE has been mandated the role of technical agency for 14 clusters in khadi, village industry and coir sector. IIE has conducted a series of seminars/workshops covering various aspects of the implementation of the programme. In addition, IIE has also facilitated linkage with various professional and support institutions for planned capacity building activities for different clusters. IIE has assisted the implementing agencies in product development both through design development and technology infusion by providing linkages with designers, technologists and institutions like weavers service centres etc. For market promotion, IIE has assisted the different clusters through initiatives like development of e-portal, conducting and facilitating buyer-seller meets, facilitating exhibition participation, providing linkages with marketing experts and retail houses etc.

3.2 Development and Training Institutes for Micro, Small and Medium Enterprises (MSMEs)

3.2.1 National Institute for Micro, Small and Medium Enterprises (NI-MSME), Hyderabad: See section 3.1.1 of this chapter.

3.2.2 Other Development Institutes for MSMEs:

A. MSME Development Institutes (MSME-DIs): The network of 30 MSME-DIs and 28 Branch MSME-DIs, set up in the State capitals and other industrial cities all over the country, mainly performs the following functions:

1. Organizing industrial motivation campaign/entrepreneurship, management and skill development programmes.
2. Assistance/consultancy to prospective and existing entrepreneurs.
3. Preparing state and district industrial potential survey reports.
4. Preparation/updation of project profiles of products/industries suitable and feasible in the MSMEs sector.
5. Conducting energy conservation, pollution control, quality control and upgradation.
6. Assisting ancillary development.
7. Making available common facility services in workshops and laboratories.
8. Preparation of directory of specific industries.
9. Market surveys.
10. Coordination with DICs and linkages with State Government functionaries.

11. Promotion and handholding of micro and small enterprises under Rajiv Gandhi Udyami Mitra Yojana (RGUMY).

B. MSME Tool Rooms (MSME-TRs): In present day fast-paced global business scenario, technology has become more vital than ever before. With a view to foster the growth of MSMEs, Government has set up tool rooms and training centres. These tool rooms provide valuable service to the Indian industry by way of precision tooling and providing well-trained craftsmen in the area of tool and die making. These tool rooms are highly proficient in mould and die making technology and promote precision and quality in the development and manufacture of sophisticated moulds, dies and tools. The tool room and training centres also offer various training programmes to meet the wide spectrum of technical manpower required in the manufacturing sector. The training programmes are designed with optimum blend of theory and practice giving the trainees exposure on actual jobs and hands on working experience. The tool rooms have also developed special training programmes to meet the requirements at international level, which are attended by participants from all over the globe.

The 10 MSME-TRs, set up under the Indo-German and Indo-Danish collaborations, assist MSMEs in technical upgradation and provide good quality tooling through designing and producing tools, moulds, jigs and fixtures, components etc. These tool rooms also provide technical training and consultancy in the area of tool and die making. The names and locations of different tool rooms are as under:

1. MSME-Tool Room (Central Tool Room), Ludhiana.
2. MSME-Tool Room (Indo-German Tool Room), Ahmedabad.
3. MSME-Tool Room (Indo-German Tool Room), Indore.
4. MSME-Tool Room (Indo-German Tool Room), Aurangabad.
5. MSME-Tool Room (Central Tool Room and Training Centre), Kolkata.
6. MSME-Tool Room (Central Tool Room and Training Centre), Bhubaneswar.

7. MSME-Tool Room (Indo-Danish Tool Room), Jamshedpur.
8. MSME-Tool Room (Central Institute of Hand Tools), Jalandhar.
9. MSME-Tool Room (Central Institute of Tool Design), Hyderabad.
10. MSME-Tool Room (Hand Tool Design and Training Centre), Nagaur.

C. MSME Technology Development Centres (MSME-TDCs): These are product-specific centres for addressing product-specific problems and rendering technical services, developing and upgrading technologies and manpower development and training in respective product groups like foundry and forging, electronics, fragrance and flavour, sport shoes, electrical measuring instruments and glass.

Names and locations of different MSME-TDCs are as under:

1. Electronics Service and Training Centre (ESTC), Ramnagar.
2. Institute for Design of Electrical Measuring Instruments (IDEMI), Mumbai.
3. Fragrance and Flavour Development Centre (FFDC), Kannauj.
4. Centre for Development of Glass Industry (CDGI), Firozabad.
5. Process and Product Development Centre (PPDC), Agra.
6. Process-cum-Product Development Centre (PPDC), Meerut.

The main objective of MSME-TDCs is to develop human resources for meeting the requirements for transfer of technology in respective products fields. Some of them are also running training courses as per the requirements of the industry. The CDGI, Firozabad provides technical support to micro and small glass units through promoting installation of energy efficient glass melting furnaces, auxiliary furnaces, introduction of new types of glasses and their standardization, introduction of developed techniques for the decoration of glasswares etc.

D. MSME Testing Centres (MSME-TCs): These centres located in Chennai, Delhi, Kolkata and Mumbai have facilities for quality upgradation, training/consultancy in testing, quality control, quality management, process quality control systems etc.

MSME-TCs provide testing and calibration facilities to industries in general and MSMEs in particular for raw materials, semi-finished and finished products, manufactured by them. The centres are equipped with the state-of-the-art indigenous and imported equipment in the field of chemical, mechanical, metallurgical and electrical engineering to undertake performance tests, type tests and acceptance tests of semi-finished, finished products etc. The centres also undertake calibration works for measuring instruments and equipment conforming to international standards. These centres are accredited by internationally recognized National Accreditation Board of Testing and Calibration Laboratories (NABL) certification as per ISO (17025).

E. MSME Testing Stations (MSME-TSs): In order to provide testing facilities in the area with cluster of industries and some strategic areas, MSME-TSs have been set up in Jaipur, Bhopal, Kolhapur, Hyderabad, Bengaluru, Puducherry and Ettumanur. These testing stations extend facilities for testing of various products, viz. chemicals, dye-stuffs, lamps, rubber products, castings and forgings, paints and varnishes, domestic electrical appliances, general engineering etc.

These testing stations in fact act as extensions of MSME-TCs thereby serving the needs of the industries situated in far-flung areas.

F. MSME Technology Development Centres (Central Footwear Training Institutes) (MSME-TDCs-CFTI): These centres located in Agra and Chennai are engaged in developing designs and development of footwear and also providing training for skill development to footwear industry.

The basic objective of these centres is to develop human resources for footwear and allied industries through various training programmes on footwear technology and allied services. These centres conduct long-term, short-term and part-time training courses on different subjects of footwear technology. Besides, they provide technical support services to the user industry through making their facilities available to them. They also provide services for development of new products and patterns as per given sample or concept.

In short, the institutional and legal framework for promotion and development of micro, small and medium enterprises (MSMEs) sector of India is spread both at the national and state level. The primary responsibility for the development of MSMEs lies with the State Governments. Government of India supplements their efforts through a range of initiatives. The employment-intensive MSMEs sector has suffered extensively due to plethora of laws, rules and regulations that have accumulated during the years of control regime. Ensuring compliance with so many regulations coupled with *Inspector Raj* has stifled growth of the sector considerably.

The district industries centres under State Governments and MSME Development Institutes of Ministry of MSMEs provide facilitation to the new and existing entrepreneurs in developing their enterprises. With the implementation of Micro, Small and Medium Enterprises Development (MSMED) Act, 2006, two new sectors were classified in the country, i.e. medium sector and service sector, which required special attention for promotion and growth as these sectors were identified for the first time in any statute.

Introduction of filing of entrepreneurs memorandum under the MSMED Act was an important initiative towards liberalisation of the MSMEs sector. This provision liberated the entrepreneurs from the hurdles of registration of enterprises required under previous policy regime, for availing institutional finance and infrastructural support.

Provision of the delayed payment under the MSMED Act was another facilitator for ensuring regular cash flow to micro and small enterprises against the supplies made. Micro and small enterprises facilitation councils (MSEFCs) stipulated under the Act to be set up at the State level were foreseen as facilitators to the MSEs. However, most of these MSEFCs are not operating efficiently. In fact, in some states they are yet to be constituted.

Endnotes

1. National Institute for Entrepreneurship and Small Business Development (NIESBUD) was transferred to Ministry of Skill Development and Entrepreneurship (MSDE) on May 2, 2015.
2. Indian Institute of Entrepreneurship (IIE), Guwahati was transferred to Ministry of Skill Development and Entrepreneurship (MSDE) on May 2, 2015.

4

Schemes for Entrepreneurship Development

4.1 Rajiv Gandhi Udyami Mitra Yojana (RGUMY)

World over, micro and small enterprises (MSEs) are recognized as an important/constituent of the national economies, contributing significantly to employment expansion and poverty alleviation. Recognizing the importance of micro and small enterprises, which constitute an important segment of Indian economy in terms of their contribution to country's industrial production, exports, employment and creation of entrepreneurial base, the Central and State Governments have been implementing several schemes and programmes for promotion and development of these enterprises.

The small scale industries in India, including the tiny or micro industries and service/business entities, collectively referred as micro and small enterprises (MSEs), have a long history of promoting inclusive, spatially widespread and employment-oriented economic growth. In terms of employment generation, this segment is next only to agriculture.

Entrepreneurship development and training is one of the key elements for development and promotion of micro and small enterprises, particularly, the first generation entrepreneurs. Entrepreneurship development programmes (EDPs) of various durations are being organized on regular basis by a number of organizations e.g. national and state level entrepreneurship development institutes (EDIs), micro, small and medium enterprises development institutes (MSMEDIs) [earlier known as small industries service institutes (SISIs)], national and state level industrial development corporations, banks and other training institutions/agencies in private and public sector etc., to create new entrepreneurs by cultivating their latent qualities of entrepreneurship and enlightening them on various aspects necessary for setting up micro and small enterprises. Besides, various industrial training institutes (ITIs), other private training institutions are also organizing vocational training (VT) programmes, skill development programmes (SDPs) and entrepreneurship-cum-skill development programmes (ESDPs).

However, there are still wide spread variations in the success rate, in terms of actual setting up and successful running of enterprises, by the EDP/SDP/ESDP trained entrepreneurs. It has been observed that entrepreneurs particularly new entrepreneurs, generally face difficulties in availing full benefits under available schemes of the Governments/financial institutions, completing and complying with various formalities and legal requirements under various laws/regulations, in selection of appropriate technology, tie-up with buyers and sellers etc. In order to bridge the gap between the aspirations of the potential entrepreneurs and the ground realties, there is a need to support and nurture the potential first generation as well as existing entrepreneurs by giving them handholding support, particularly during the initial stages of setting up and managing their enterprises.

In order to improve the success rate of the entrepreneurship development programme (EDP) trainees in the establishment of new enterprises, the Ministry of MSMEs launched a scheme, namely *Rajiv Gandhi Udyami Mitra Yojana* (a scheme for Promotion and Handholding of Micro and Small Enterprises). The main objective of this scheme is to provide handholding support to first generation entrepreneurs through designated lead agencies, i.e. *Udyami Mitras*. Under this scheme, the *Udyami Mitras* are providing guidance and assistance to the potential entrepreneurs registered with them in: (a) preparation of project reports, (b) arrangement of finance, (c) selection of technology, (d) marketing tie-ups with buyers, (e) installation of plant and machinery, and (f) obtaining various approvals, clearances etc. For providing this handholding assistance to the new entrepreneurs, the *Udyami Mitras* are paid handholding charges under the scheme, including nominal contribution of the concerned entrepreneur. However, the beneficiaries belonging to SCs, STs, physically handicapped and women are subsidized under the scheme for availing the handholding support from *Udyami Mitra*.

4.1.1 Objectives of RGUMY: These are as under:

1. To provide handholding support and assistance to the potential first generation entrepreneurs, who have already successfully completed or undergoing entrepreneurship development training programme (EDP)/skill development training programme (SDP)/entrepreneurship-cum-skill development training programme (ESDP)/vocation training programmes (VT), through the selected lead agencies i.e. *Udyami Mitras*, in the establishment and management of the new enterprise, in dealing with various procedural and legal hurdles and in completion of various formalities required for setting up and running of the enterprise.
2. To provide information, support, guidance and assistance to first generation entrepreneurs and other existing entrepreneurs through *Udyami Helpline* (a call centre for MSMEs), to guide them regarding various promotional schemes of the Government, procedural formalities required for setting up and running of the enterprise and help them in accessing bank credit etc.

4.1.2 Udyami Mitras:

A. Eligibility: Under RGUMY, financial assistance would be provided to the selected lead agencies, i.e. *Udyami Mitras* for rendering assistance and handholding support to the potential first generation entrepreneurs. Following agencies and organizations can be appointed as the lead agency, i.e. *Udyami Mitra*:

1. Existing national level entrepreneurship development institutions (EDIs).
2. Micro, small and medium enterprises development institutes (MSMEDIs)/branch MSMEDIs.
3. Central/State Government public sector enterprises (PSEs) involved in promotion and development of MSEs e.g. National Small Industries Corporation (NSIC) and State

Industrial Development Corporations etc.

4. Selected State level EDIs and entrepreneurship development centres (EDCs) in public or private sectors.
5. Khadi and Village Industries Commission (KVIC).
6. Special purpose vehicles (SPVs) set up for cluster development involved in entrepreneurship development.
7. Capable associations of MSEs/SSIs.
8. Other organizations/training institutions/NGOs etc. involved in entrepreneurship development/skill development.

B. Role and Responsibilities of *Udyami Mitras*: The selected lead agencies i.e. *Udyami Mitras* would be expected to render assistance and handholding support for following services:

1. Networking, coordinating and follow up with various Government departments, agencies, organizations and regulatory agencies on the one hand and with support agencies like banks/financial institutions, district industries centres (DICs), technology providers, infrastructure providers on the other hand, to help the first generation entrepreneurs in setting up their enterprise. *Udyami Mitras* are expected to help the first generation entrepreneurs in the following manner:

- Identification of suitable project/product/enterprise and preparation of bankable project report for the same.
- Creation of the proprietorship firm, partnership firm, company, society, self-help group (SHG) etc.
- Filing of memorandum (as prescribed under MSMED Act, 2006).
- Accessing bank loans, admissible capital subsidy/assistance under various schemes of the Central/State Government and other agencies, organizations, financial institutions, banks etc. by networking with respective agencies.
- Assistance and support in establishment of work shed/office.
- Sanction of power load/connection.
- Selection of appropriate technology and installation of plant and machinery and office equipment etc.

- Obtaining various registrations, licenses, clearances and no objection certificates (NOCs).
- NOCs from the concerned regulatory agencies, Government departments, local bodies, municipal authorities etc.
- Allotment of income tax permanent account number (PAN) and service tax/sales tax/VAT registration etc.
- Sanction of working capital loan from the banks.
- Arranging tie up with raw material suppliers.
- Preparation and implementation of marketing strategy for the product/service and market development.
- Establishing linkage with a mentor for providing guidance in future.
- Creation of web page and email identity.

2. Once the enterprise has been successfully set up, the *Udyami Mitras* would also monitor and follow up on the functioning of the enterprise for a further period of minimum 6 months and provide help in overcoming various managerial, financial and operational problems.

4.2 India Aspiration Fund (IAF)

In August 2015, Government launched IAF to be set up as a fund of funds under the Small Industries Development Bank of India (SIDBI) in order to boost the start-up ecosystem in the country.

The objective of IAF is to catalyse tens of thousands of crores of equity investment into start-ups and micro, small and medium enterprises (MSMEs) creating employment of lakhs of persons, mostly educated youth, over the next four to five years.

India is witnessing a start-up revolution and to harness the potential of India's innovators and entrepreneurs, a vibrant financial ecosystem is essential. IAF will play a vital role in this financial ecosystem.

This is a well-structured fund and since it is built on sectoral allocations, it will provide investment to start-ups in sectors which are not hot today for venture funds but will become hot in future.

SIDBI under the IAF would invest in venture capital funds for meeting the equity requirement of MSME start-ups. Hence, instead of directly funding in start-ups, IAF will help the venture capitals to come up with newer investment ideas and protocols. Besides infusing crores of funding into MSMEs, this will also create lakhs of new jobs. For this, the initial corpus of ₹ 2,000 crore has been set. Life Insurance Corporation of India (LIC) will be a partner and co-investor in this fund.

The IAF will be managed by an investment committee composed of captains of industry and finance.

4.3 SIDBI Make in India Loan for Small Enterprises (SMILE)

See section 7.5.1 of chapter 7 of this book.

4.4 Self-Employment and Talent Utilisation (SETU)

See section 7.5.3 of chapter 7 of this book.

5

Women Empowerment through Entrepreneurship

Women-owned businesses are increasing in the economies of almost all the countries. The hidden entrepreneurial potential of women has gradually been changing with the growing sensitivity towards the role and economic status in the society.

5.1 Why Women Empowerment?

The extent of empowerment of women in the national hierarchy is determined largely by three factors: their economic, social and political identity. These factors are deeply intertwined and interlinked with many cross-cutting linkages. However, if efforts in even one dimension remain absent or weak, outcomes generated by the other components are adversely affected. Women can be truly empowered only when all the three factors are simultaneously addressed and made compatible with each other. In other words, for holistic empowerment of women to happen, economic, social and political aspects impacting women's life must converge effectively.

It is a well-acknowledged fact that the thrust on social and human development is an important plank of next generation policy reforms. The efforts are being complemented by a steep jump in budgetary outlays for social sectors, along with dedicated initiatives for removing poverty and increasing employment. Participation of women in productive activities reduces poverty, enhances economic growth and hence benefits society at large.

Women's lack of economic empowerment not only impedes growth and poverty reduction, but also has a host of other negative impacts including less favourable education and health outcomes for children. Thus, it is extremely important to ensure that women are economically empowered.

Women's contribution to the economy remains significantly invisible in national accounts. Although a certain degree of statistical invisibility of women in the economy is a global phenomenon, it is particularly predominant in India and other South Asian nations due to their orthodox socio-cultural milieu. The United Nations Statistical Division has been active in extending the production boundary of the Systems of National Accounts (SNA), 1993 and this has led to the inclusion of the unpaid work of women in the care economy in the national accounting system as satellite accounts. This extended production boundary of SNA, 1993 provides a better understanding of women's contribution to the economy.

5.2 Changing Role of Women in Modern Societies

Apart from agriculture, women in India are mostly employed in manufacturing activities. In addition, the process of *feminization* has been fastest in the manufacturing sector. A substantial part of this is in the form of employment in micro and small enterprises (MSEs), especially in the household enterprises.

In the traditional society, a woman's role was naturally limited to the family. Since she was the beam of children, she was fully occupied with her duties as a mother and home maker. This was no small feat, since the traditional household may be described as both a production and a consumption unit. A man's responsibility was to provide the household with the raw materials which were then converted by the woman into consumable products under precarious housing conditions and by means of rudimentary methods and tools.

The role of women has been changing substantially over the recent past, both inside and outside the homes. In addition to their role within the household, they are now having a larger role in the outside world also, especially in the labour market. It has often been argued that women face a segmented labour market with sector-specific jobs and often gender-specific wages assigned to them. However, the world is witnessing a significant change in this traditional thinking regarding the ability of women to work only in a few specific sectors. Gone are the days when women were employed mostly as low paid casual workers in agricultural and construction activities.

Many factors like urbanization, technical progress, education etc. have profoundly changed these traditional conditions even in a developing country like India. A woman's role at home has become lighter due to the technical progress.

Mechanization and automation of many production processes have decreased the importance of a man's physical ability over woman for performing a physical job. Further, it has not been scientifically proved that a woman is incomparable to a man either in skill or mental abilities. This has enabled women to take advantage of the industrialisation process. The very process of urbanisation and industrialisation has led to a consumer society, where many desirable products are readily available. Women perceive more and more clearly that if they really want to contribute to the welfare of their family and society the most effective way is to go out of home and earn money.

The recent emphasis and perception is that women can also contribute to the economy of the nation as workers and producers, social scientists, policy makers and administrators. Government has also been implementing schemes and programmes to ensure the development of women.

5.3 From 3 Ks to 3 Ps to 4 Es

To begin with, women were confined to the four walls of the household to look after the requirements of the family. It all revolved around the following 3 Ks:

1. Kitchen.
2. Kids.
3. Knitting.

The situation converted into the following 3 Ps towards the

closing years of the 20th century:

1. Powder.
2. Pappad.
3. Pickles.

Presently, the trend is towards the following 4 Es:

1. Electricity.
2. Electronics.
3. Energy.
4. Engineering.

In spite of all these, women still find themselves at the receiving end in the labour market. Women are dependant on informal sector more heavily than men, and as a result, their share in this sector is higher than their share in total labour force. Even within the informal sector, most of the women are own account workers or home-based workers. However, this traditional setting is changing, albeit slowly, and the share of women in wage employment is increasing along with the intrusion of more and more women into hitherto male bastions.

5.4 Women Entrepreneurship

An entrepreneur is a person who is able to scan the environment, marshal resources and implement actions to bring into existence a commercial venture, and can initiate and establish large, medium or small enterprises. The concept of women entrepreneurship is multidisciplinary in nature embodying economic, psychological, social, cultural and political as well as environmental characteristics. The types of responses women are generating in certain circumstances highlight women as special type of entrepreneurs, away from men with distinction. The need for bringing women to the mainstream of economic development is because of their proven success in all fields, wherever they got the opportunity. Traditionally, women, be it mother, wife or sister, used to be in-charge of the household management. Although, over the last few decades women have come forward to establish their own enterprises, yet their number remains small in a male-dominated world. Women's work, however innovative it might be, goes unrecognized.

Women entrepreneurs may be defined as the women or a group of women who initiate, organize and operate a business enterprise. The Government of India has defined women entrepreneurs as an enterprise owned and controlled by women having a minimum financial interest of 51 percent of the capital and giving at least 51 percent of the employment generated in the enterprise to women. A sense of independent decision-making is the motivational factor behind this urge. Saddled with household chores and domestic responsibilities, women want to get independence. Under the influence of these factors, women entrepreneurs choose a profession as a challenge and as an urge to do something new. Such a situation is described as pull factors. Push factors pertain to women engaged in business activities due to family compulsions and/or family responsibilities.

Women entrepreneurs in India represent a group of women who have broken away from the beaten track and are exploring new vistas of economic participation. They have long stories of struggle and hardships. Their task has been full of challenges. They have encountered public prejudices, family opposition and social constraints. Women entrepreneurs perform just like any other male entrepreneur. To be successful in the field of entrepreneurship, a woman needs to exhibit the traits, which are very much needed to compete and bear the pressure of business enterprises.

Several factors influence women to take up entrepreneurial ventures. The economic role is largely determined by the traditional division of labour by sex where women tend to undertake and specialize in work near the home such as food processing, household maintenance, horticulture and handicrafts etc. The concept of women entrepreneurship is becoming a global phenomenon and in India it became prominent in the later half of the 1980s. There are various factors that motivate a woman to take on entrepreneurial activities. Prominently, it is not always easy for a woman to find a job that is compatible with her family responsibilities and household chores. This encourages women towards self-employment in enterprises adjoining their places of residence with flexible working hours, which allows them to take care of both home and business.

Entrepreneurship development is a very crucial factor for the acceleration of economic growth of any country and women entrepreneurship development is an essential part of human resource development. Women have started showing more interest in entrepreneurship because it provides them an opportunity to be their own boss.

5.5 Characteristics of Women Entrepreneurs

Woman entrepreneurs tend to be highly motivated and self-directed. They also exhibit a high internal locus of control and achievement. Researchers contend that women business owners possess certain specific characteristics that promote their creativity and generate new ideas and ways of doing things.

Women entrepreneurs share the following characteristics:

1. Sharp communication skills.
2. Intuitive skills.
3. Consensus building competencies.
4. Nurturing and integrating abilities.

Women need to use all these skills as they strive to make appropriate decisions for their families and for themselves.

With the advent of media, women are aware of their own traits, rights and also the work situations. The challenges and opportunities provided to the women of digital era are growing rapidly—the job seekers are turning into job creators. Many women start a business due to some traumatic event, such as divorce, discrimination due to pregnancy or the corporate glass ceiling, the health of a family member, or economic reasons such as a layoff. However, a new talent pool of women entrepreneurs is forming today, as more women opt to leave the corporate world to chart their own destinies. They are flourishing as designers, interior decorators, exporters, publishers, garment manufacturers and still exploring new avenues of economic participation.

5.6 Preferable Areas of Business Enterprise for Women

Business opportunities for women are growing in the following areas:

1. Eco-friendly technology
2. Bio-technology.
3. IT-enabled enterprises.
4. Event management.
5. Tourism industry.
6. Telecommunications.
7. Plastic materials.
8. Mineral water.
9. Sericulture.
10. Floriculture.
11. Herbal and healthcare.
12. Food, fruits and vegetable processing.

Empowering women entrepreneurs is essential for achieving the goals of sustainable development and the bottlenecks hindering their growth must be eradicated to ensure their full participation in the business world.

5.7 Constraints Faced by Women

Women in advanced nations are recognized and are more prominent in the business world. However, the Indian women entrepreneurs are facing some major constraints which are detailed below:

1. **Lack of Confidence:** In general, women lack confidence in their strength and competence. The family members and the society are reluctant to stand besides their entrepreneurial growth. Though this situation is changing yet women face a tremendous challenge to build their confidence.

2. **Socio-cultural Barriers:** Family and personal obligations are sometimes a formidable barrier for success in business career for women. Only few women are able to manage both home and business efficiently.
3. **Market-oriented Risks:** Stiff competition in the market and lack of mobility of women make the dependence of women entrepreneurs on middleman indispensable. Many business women find it difficult to capture the market and make their products popular. They are not fully aware of the changing market conditions and hence cannot effectively utilize the services of media and the internet.
4. **Motivational Factors:** Self-motivation can be realized through a mind set for a successful business, attitude to take up risk and behaviour towards the business society by shouldering the social responsibilities. Other factors are family support, government policies, financial assistance from public and private institutions and also the environment suitable for women to establish business units.
5. **Knowledge in Business Administration:** Women must be educated and trained constantly to acquire the skills and knowledge in all the functional areas of business management. This can facilitate women to excel in decision-making process and develop a good business network.
6. **Lack of Awareness about Financial Assistance:** Various institutions in the financial sector extend their support in the form of loans and other business promotional schemes. Women entrepreneurs are generally not aware of all these programmes/schemes. Benefits of such schemes do not reach women entrepreneurs, particularly in rural and backward areas.
7. **Lack of Exposure to Training Programmes:** Various training programmes and workshops for every type of entrepreneur are being organized by the Central and State Governments. Such programs are useful to new, rural and young entrepreneurs who want to set up a small-scale units on their own. However, not all potential women

entrepreneurs are aware of these facilities.

8. **Identifying the Available Resources:** Women are hesitant to find out facilities in financial and marketing areas. In spite of the mushrooming growth of associations, institutions, and schemes, women are not dynamic enough to optimize resources in the form of reserves and assets.

Highly educated, technically sound and professionally qualified women should be encouraged for managing their own businesses, rather than being dependant on wage employment outlets. The unexplored talents of young women can be identified, trained and used for various types of industries to increase the productivity in the industrial sector. A desirable environment is necessary for every woman to inculcate entrepreneurial values and involve in business dealings.

5.8 Women Entrepreneurship in Global Context

Entrepreneurship emerges from an individual's creative spirit into long-term business ownership, job creation, and economic security. Women bring commitment and integrity because they care about economic empowerment, entrepreneurial development and innovation. Female entrepreneurs seek the professional and personal support that is found in business associations. Economic globalization has encouraged the expansion of female business ownership.

Moreover, it is often argued that globalization is leading to feminization of labour force through sub-contracting as employing women under informal conditions involves lower labour cost. It is also believed that such feminization is the result of growing flexibility in the labour market whereby women find themselves in traditionally male-dominated jobs.

With the growing globalization and liberalization of the economy as well as increased privatization of services, women as a whole have been left behind and not been able to partake the fruits of success. Mainstreaming of women into the new and emerging areas of growth is imperative. This will require training and skill upgradation in emerging trades, and encouraging more women to take up vocational training and employment in the boom sectors. This will also require women to migrate to cities and metros for work. Provision of safe housing, and other gender-friendly facilities at work will need to be provided.

Another facet of globalization is related to the fact that many persons especially women will be severely affected with the advent of setting up of industrial parks, national highways, special economic zones (SEZs) etc. as huge tracts of farm land are likely to be acquired for this purpose. This would require massive resettlement of the displaced persons and their families. It is, therefore, essential that a viable resettlement policy and strategy is formulated and put in place immediately which clearly reflects the needs of women impacted by globalization/displacement.

With the removal of all quantitative restrictions on the import of various products, the self-employed women groups, especially in the informal sector, have started facing competition from the low-priced imported consumer goods which are invading the Indian market. Although this has the imminent danger of displacing a large number of employed/self-employed women, but at the same time, the process of globalization has also opened up opportunities for women entrepreneurs for exporting their products to the markets all over the world. Globalization has thus opened up new challenges for the realization of the goal of women's empowerment. Hence, strategies should be designed to enhance the capacity of women and empower them to cope with the negative economic and social impacts of the globalization process.

Several studies have indicated that adverse consequences of globalisation are disproportionately borne by women. Increased mechanization leading to displacement of female unskilled workers, increased migration of male workers in traditionally women-dominated areas, increase in female-headed households due to migration of males are some of the trends established in various studies.

Globalization has presented new challenges for the realization of the goal of women's equality, the gender impact of which has not been systematically evaluated fully. However, it is evident that there is a need for re-framing policies for access to employment and equality of employment. Benefits of the growing global economy have been unevenly distributed leading to wider economic disparities, the feminization of poverty, increased gender inequality through deteriorating working conditions and unsafe working environment especially in the informal economy and rural areas. Strategies need to be designed to enhance the capacity of women and empower them to meet the negative social and economic impacts, which may flow from the globalization process.

With upgradation of skills, opportunities for employment of women exist in several areas such as health services, food processing and crafts. Key areas of concern include women in small subsistence farming households, women workers in garment and textiles who will face increased competition after the phasing out of the Multi Fibre Agreement in 2005, and women displaced by new technologies in sectors such as construction, which have traditionally absorbed a large number of women.

With the onset of trade liberalisation, women in India today are linked with the global economy to a very significant extent, as producers, entrepreneurs, service providers, consumers and citizens. There is a need to identify capacity constraints and entry barriers that prevent women from securing gains from trade. Trade-related awareness and capacity building of the women stakeholders need to be prioritised.

The globalization process has, in some countries, resulted in policy shifts in favour of more open trade and financial flows, privatization of state-owned enterprises and in many cases lower public spending, particularly on social services. This change has transformed patterns of production and accelerated technological advances in information and communication and has affected the lives of women, both as workers and consumers. In a large number of countries, particularly in developing and least developed countries, these changes have also adversely impacted the lives of women and have increased inequality. The gender impact of these changes has not been systematically evaluated. Globalization has also affected cultural values, lifestyles and forms of communication.

In countries with economies in transition, women are bearing most of the hardships induced by the economic restructuring and being the first to lose jobs in times of recession. They are being squeezed out from fast growth sectors. Loss of childcare facilities due to elimination or privatization of state work places, increased need for older care without the corresponding facilities, continuing inequality of access to training for finding re-employment and to productive assets for entering or expanding businesses are the current challenges facing women in these countries.

6

Jobs Creation: Policy and Current Scenario

6.1 Labour Policy and Productivity

Labour enters the production process from the supply side as well as from the demand side. The focal point for both aspects is higher productivity because it is through higher productivity that higher real wages can be ensured, cost of production can be brought down and higher demand for products can be generated, which would lead to further growth. The role of labour has to be perceived in this broad perspective.

The success of labour policy has to be adjudged on the basis of the productivity standard that it helps the economy to achieve. While technical factors and the state of technology are crucial in determining productivity levels, there is no denying the fact that discipline and motivation of workers, their skill, the state of industrial relations, the extent and effectiveness of participation of workers, the working climate and safety practices are also of great importance. While maximising employment generation, requisite attention has to be directed to the improvement of labour productivity through the adoption of up-to-date technology in productive processes in major sectors and corrective measures for industrial sickness.

Labour policy in India has been evolving in response to the specific needs of the situation in relation to industry and the working class and has to suit the requirements of a planned economy. A body of principles and practices has grown up as a product of joint consultation in which representatives of Government, the working class and employers have been participating at various levels. The legislative and other measures adopted by the Central and State Governments in this field represent the consensus of opinion of the parties concerned and thus acquire the strength and character of a national policy.

Under various laws, a comprehensive code has been developed to ensure satisfactory working conditions, safety of person and the provision of a variety of facilities to promote the welfare of the workers. Steps, however, have to be taken to make the implementation of the statutory provisions more effective. The improvement of working conditions can result in greater productive efficiency on the part of the workers. Every effort should be made to keep abreast of the modern developments in these and various other aspects relating to the human factor in industry. The problem of safety should receive greater attention.

6.2 Jobs Generation Strategy

Progressive reduction of unemployment has been one of the principal objectives of economic planning in India. It has been envisaged that the growth of the economy would not only increase production but also provide the capacity for absorbing the backlog of unemployment and under-employment and a substantial proportion of the additions to the labour force. The solution to the problem of unemployment—and the poverty that goes with it—has to be found ultimately through a high rate of overall economic growth. It is, therefore, necessary to have supplemental programmes for specific target groups/areas for employment creation, income generation and poverty alleviation. These have taken the form of direct employment programmes for providing seasonal employment to the agricultural labourers on rural capital works and infrastructure creation.

Consistent with the approach for an employment-centred development strategy, public employment programmes are an integral part of planning and policy. Apart from the advantages that accrue to the unemployed, under-employed and the poorly-employed, such programmes have a positive macroeconomic impact via increase in effective demand from the hitherto poor and vulnerable segments of the population.

Employment generation as an objective does not mean the adoption of a static technology. It is not advisable to insulate the economy from the world trends in technological changes. Technological upgradation, modernisation and scientific advances in production process constitute the essence of growth of productivity whether it is in organised industry, agriculture or small industry. A clear view of efficiency and employment effects downstream should be formulated before setting about the management of technological change. There must be suitable arrangements and adjustment policies in terms of education, training and retraining and re-orientation of workers in order to avoid dislocation effects and make the process of technology adoption smooth.

In formulating the employment strategy, a key role has to be assigned to the growth of the agricultural sector. A steady growth in agricultural production through the expansion of irrigation, increase in cropping intensity and the extension of new agricultural technologies to low productivity regions could create a large volume of additional employment. However, the agricultural sector alone cannot be expected to eliminate the backlog of unemployment and absorb the additions to the labour force. The rate of industrial growth must be accelerated.

However, as experience has shown, even a high rate of industrial growth would not be able to create additional employment to absorb more than a fraction of the unemployed and under-employed labour force in the organised industrial sector. Therefore, programmes of rural development and, in particular, of massive rural capital formation in the form of construction become necessary. This strategy would also help raise the rate of growth of agriculture. Further, it would increase the income of the weaker segments of the population and thereby provide the demand support to the growth process.

The problem of the educated unemployed raises special issues. It has to be tackled through proper educational planning and schemes of training, skill formation and entrepreneurial development.

The expansion of employment that ensures adequate livelihood security and decent conditions of work ought to be the bottom line in the pursuit of economic development in a country like India dominated by what is called the informal economy.

6.3 Direct Employment Programmes

Programmes to create direct employment opportunities for wage workers through public works have in the past focused on generation of supplementary employment opportunities, especially during lean periods. They have been considered as an important component of the anti-poverty strategy. These programmes are expected to create durable assets for the community and thus enhance further economic activities. Wage employment programmes also push up demand for labour and thus exert an upward pressure on the market wage rates by attracting people to public works programmes, thereby reducing supply of cheap labour, often at wages that would not even meet their bare basic needs.

Consistent with the approach for an employment-centred development strategy, public employment programmes are seen as an integral part of planning and policy. Apart from the advantages that would accrue to the unemployed, under-employed and the poorly-employed, such programmes have a positive macroeconomic impact via increase in effective demand from the hitherto poor and vulnerable segments of the population.

Past experiences show that India's poverty alleviation strategy—including the National Rural Employment Programme (NREP), Rural Labour Employment Guarantee Programme (RLEGP), Jawahar Rojgar Yojana (JRY), Employment Assurance Scheme (EAS), Sampoorna Gramin Rojgar Yojana (SGRY)—leaned towards wage employment programmes.

The rationale for adopting wage employment programmes by the Government during the last many decades has been that they provide steady opportunities for employment to those who are unemployed or underemployed. Beneficiaries include those who have labour as the only asset under their control (owning neither capital nor skills), and are unable to take even the minimal risks associated with self-employment. State assistance in the form of such wage employment then acts as a valuable safeguard against risks and vulnerabilities. Other positive externalities of wage employment programmes include the upward pressure on market wages because of the higher wages from the government programmes and organizing the rural poor beneficiaries of the schemes into collectives.

The solution of the problem of unemployment lies in reversing the causes of unemployment. It means controlling the population growth, speeding up the pace of industrialisation, adoption of labour-intensive technology and making the education system job-oriented.

Since the initiation of reforms in early 1990s, many changes have taken place in the social life and the institutions that govern the economy. In science and technology, information system and communications, revolutionary changes have occurred in recent times. New ideas have emerged which have changed the way people all over the world look at old ideas and the old institutions.

To deal with the unemployment problem, Government of India has launched, from time to time, various employment schemes. Huge amounts of public money are being spent on recurring annual basis to support wage employment programmes. A constant monitoring of these programmes is necessary to evaluate their contribution to employment generation vis-à-vis expenditure incurred on them.

6.4 Is India's Growth Jobless?

This question is best answered by the following observation of NITI Aayog, "Contrary to some assertions that India's growth has been *jobless*, the Employment- Unemployment Surveys (EUSs) of the National Sample Survey Office (NSSO), which till date remain the most reliable sources of information on India's employment situation, have consistently reported low and stable rates of unemployment over more than three decades.

Even under the most demanding definition of employment, the unemployment rate consistently remains between 5 percent and 8 percent.

Indeed, unemployment is the lesser of India's problems. The more serious problem, instead, is severe underemployment. A job that one worker can perform is often performed by two or more workers. In effect, those in the workforce are employed, but they are overwhelmingly stuck in low-productivity, low-wage jobs.

Therefore, what is needed is the creation of high-productivity, high-wage jobs. Accordingly, focus should be on the measures necessary for the increased emergence of larger, organized-sector firms. The experience of countries that managed to transform rapidly, such as South Korea, Taiwan, Singapore and China, shows that the manufacturing sector and the ability to compete in the vast global marketplace hold the key to the creation of well-paid jobs for low and semi-skilled workers.

India has, of course, already achieved considerable success in some key services and skilled-labour-intensive industries. It has had great success in the global markets in information technology (IT), information technology-enabled services (ITES) and pharmaceuticals. Its financial sector, including capital markets, has also acquired a modern character and has been exhibiting healthy growth during the past one and a half decades.

A large part of India's population resides in rural areas. The challenges in the rural areas include creating jobs such that some agricultural workers could shift to non-farm sectors, skill development, accessing education and health facilities, infrastructure, local governance, drinking water and sanitation and financial inclusion". [1]

While improvement in the overall growth performance has a direct bearing for faster and better quality employment generation, equally important is the sectoral structure of the growth. To the extent a larger share of growth can be derived from labour-intensive sectors/sub-sectors/industries, the pace of generation of employment opportunities for any given overall rate of growth can be increased. The characteristics of the different segment of the labour force in terms of their skill base, residential status, aspirations from the job etc. also have implications for the sectoral structure of growth which can most suitably and productively employ the labour force. The requirements of employment opportunities to be created for among the rural unskilled labour force on the one hand and among the educated youth on the other are different and this needs to be kept in mind.

Endnote

1. NITI Aayog, *India: Three Year Action Agenda (2017-18 to 2019-20)*, August 2017, pp. 3-4.

7

Make in India Campaign

Make in India is an initiative of the Government of India to encourage multinational, as well as domestic, companies to manufacture their products in India. It was launched by Prime Minister Shri Narendra Modi on September 25, 2014. The objective is to make India as the top destination globally for foreign direct investment.

7.1 Origin and the Roadmap

On December 29, 2014, a workshop was organised by the Department of Industrial Policy and Promotion, (DIPP), Ministry of Commerce and Industry, Government of India which was attended by Prime Minister Modi, his cabinet ministers and chief secretaries of states as well as various industry leaders.

DIPP worked with a group of highly specialised agencies to build brand new infrastructure, including a dedicated help desk and a website that packed a wide array of information into a simple, sleek menu. Designed primarily for mobile screens, the site's architecture ensured that exhaustive levels of detail are neatly tucked away so as not to overwhelm the user. 25 sector brochures were also developed which included key facts and figures, policies and initiatives and sector-specific contact details, all of which was made available in print and on site.

These exercises resulted in a road map for the single largest manufacturing initiative undertaken by a nation in recent history. They also demonstrated the transformational power of public-private partnership, and have become a hallmark of the Make in India initiative. This collaborative model has also been successfully extended to include India's global partners, as evidenced by the recent in-depth interactions between India and the United States of America.

The major objective behind the initiative is to focus on job creation and skill enhancement in 25 sectors of the economy. The initiative also aims at high quality standards and minimising the impact on the environment. Hence, the slogan *zero defect, zero effect.* The slogan also aims to prevent products developed from India from being rejected by the global market. The initiative hopes to attract capital and technological investment in India.

Before the initiative was launched, foreign equity caps in various sectors had been relaxed. The application for licenses was made available online and the validity of licenses was increased to three years. Various other norms and procedures were also relaxed.

Devised to transform India into a global design and manufacturing hub, Make in India was a timely response to a critical situation: by 2013, the much-hyped emerging markets bubble had burst, and India's growth rate had fallen to its lowest level in a decade. The promise of the BRICS Nations (Brazil, Russia, India, China and South Africa) had faded, and India was tagged as one of the so-called *Fragile Five*. Global investors debated whether the world's largest democracy was a risk or an opportunity. India's 1.2 billion citizens questioned whether India was too big to succeed or too big to fail. India was on the brink of severe economic failure.

Make in India was launched against the backdrop of this crisis, and quickly became a rallying cry for India's innumerable stakeholders and partners. It was a powerful, galvanising call to action to India's citizens and business leaders, and an invitation to potential partners and investors around the world. Make in India is much more than an inspiring slogan. It represents a comprehensive and unprecedented overhaul of out-dated processes and policies. More importantly, it represents a complete change of the Government's mindset: a shift from issuing authority to business partner.

To start a movement, a strategy is needed that inspires, empowers and enables in equal measure. Make in India needed a different kind of campaign: instead of the typical statistics-laden newspaper advertisements, this exercise required messaging that was informative, well-packaged and credible. It had to: (a) inspire confidence in India's capabilities amongst potential partners abroad, the Indian business community and citizens at large; (b) provide a framework for a vast amount of technical information on 25 industry sectors; and (c) reach out to a vast local and global audience via social media and constantly keep them updated about opportunities, reforms etc.

7.2 Four Pillars of Make in India Initiative

With the objective of making India a global hub of manufacturing, design and innovation, the Make in India initiative is based on four pillars—new processes, new infrastructure, new sectors and new mindset. The initiative is set to boost entrepreneurship, not only in manufacturing but in relevant infrastructure and service sectors as well. An interactive portal www.makeinindia.com for dissemination of information and interaction with investors has been created with the objective of generating awareness about the investment opportunities and prospects of the country, to promote India as a preferred investment destination in markets overseas and to increase Indian share of global FDI. In addition, information on 25 thrust sectors, along with details of the FDI Policy, National Manufacturing Policy, intellectual property rights and the proposed National Industrial Corridors including the Delhi Mumbai Industrial Corridor (DMIC), are available on the portal.

The Department of Industrial Policy and Promotion (DIPP), in consultation with various Central Ministries, State Governments, industry leaders, and other stakeholders, has formulated a strategy for increasing the contribution of the manufacturing sector to 25 percent of the GDP by 2020.

The Government of India has set up Invest India as the national investment promotion and facilitation agency. With the objective of promoting investment in the country, a full-fledged investment facilitation cell has been set up under the

Make in India initiative, primarily to support all investment queries as well as to handhold and liaise with various agencies on behalf of potential investors.

As envisaged by the National Manufacturing Policy, 2011, [1], Make in India seeks to create 100 million additional jobs in manufacturing by 2022. The government is taking a number of steps to enhance the skills of workers/unemployed in India in order to improve their employability. In order to tap the creative potential and boost entrepreneurship in India, the Start-up India and Stand-up India campaign have been launched. An innovation promotion platform called Atal Innovation Mission (AIM) and a techno-financial, incubation and facilitation programme called Self-Employment and Talent Utilization (SETU) are being implemented to encourage innovation and start-ups in India.

For supporting the financial needs of the small and medium enterprises sector and promote start-ups and entrepreneurship, the government has taken various steps through Make in India. The India Aspiration Fund has also been set up under the Small Industries Development Bank of India (SIDBI) for venture capital financing of newly set-up or expanding units in the MSME sector. SIDBI Make in India Loan for Small Enterprises (SMILE) has been launched to offer quasi-equity and term-based short-term loans to Indian SMEs with less stringent rules and regulations and a special focus on 25 thrust sectors of Make in India. Further, a Micro Units Development Refinance Agency (MUDRA) Bank has been set up to provide development and refinance to commercial banks/NBFCs/cooperative banks for loans given to micro-units. MUDRA Bank would follow a credit-plus approach by also providing financial literacy and addressing skill gaps, information gaps etc.

7.3 Sectors Identified

Make in India focuses on the following 25 sectors of the economy:

1. Automobiles.
2. Automobile components.
3. Aviation.
4. Biotechnology.
5. Chemicals.
6. Construction.
7. Defence manufacturing.
8. Electrical machinery.
9. Electronic systems.
10. Food processing.
11. Information technology and business process management.
12. Leather.
13. Media and entertainment.
14. Mining.
15. Oil and gas.
16. Pharmaceuticals.
17. Ports and shipping.
18. Railways.
19. Renewable energy.
20. Roads and highways.
21. Space.
22. Textiles and garments.
23. Thermal power.
24. Tourism and hospitality.
25. Wellness.

7.4 Progress of Make in India Campaign

In a short space of time, the obsolete and obstructive frameworks of the past have been dismantled and replaced with a transparent and user-friendly system that is helping drive investment, foster innovation, develop skills, protect intellectual property (IP) and build best-in-class manufacturing infrastructure. The most striking indicator of progress is the unprecedented opening up of key sectors—including railways, defence, insurance and medical devices—to dramatically higher levels of foreign direct investment (FDI).

Indian embassies and consulates have also been communicated to disseminate information on the potential for investment in the identified sectors. DIPP has set up a special management team to facilitate and fast track investment proposals from Japan, the team known as Japan Plus was operationalized in October 2014. Similarly, Korea Plus, launched in June 2016, facilitates fast track investment proposals from South Korea and offers holistic support to Korean companies wishing to enter the Indian market.

Six industrial corridors are being developed across various regions of the country. Industrial cities will also come up along these corridors.

Presently, India's credibility is stronger than ever. There is visible momentum, energy and optimism. Make in India is opening investment doors. Multiple enterprises are adopting its mantra. The world's largest democracy is well on its way to becoming the world's most powerful economy.

Make in India initiative has become a catalyst to India's booming domestic manufacturing sector. The initiative has propelled progress towards high value-added manufacturing growth and heavy investment attraction. With the help of operational and legal relaxations, effective infrastructure programmes and schemes, and focusing focus on upgrading the strength of skill sets, the Make in India initiative has facilitated the government's persistent efforts to attract investments from around the world. The initiative's aggressive efforts towards reinforcing connectivity, channelizing production methodologies, and maximizing effective investment incentives have put India on a path to excellence. Make in India is contributing to nurture the country's economic and industrial transformation, and for steering the country towards an environment conducive to domestic and global manufacturing and investment.

7.5 Make in India and Allied Schemes

7.5.1 SIDBI *Make in India* Loan Scheme for Small Enterprises (SMILE): SMILE was launched in August 2015.

The objective of SMILE scheme is to provide soft loans in the nature of quasi-equity and term loans on relatively soft terms to micro, small and medium enterprises (MSMEs). The focus of the scheme is on 25 sectors under Make in India programme with emphasis on financing smaller enterprises within the MSME sector.

SIDBI has set Initial corpus of ₹ 10,000 crore under SMILE fund.

7.5.2 Atal Innovation Mission (AIM): Finance Minister in his Budget Speech 2015-16 announced the Government's intention to establish the Atal Innovation Mission (AIM) in NITI Aayog and stated that initially a sum of ₹ 150 crore would be earmarked for this purpose. The overarching purpose of this mission is to promote a culture of entrepreneurship and innovation in India. In the years to come, entrepreneurship and innovation are expected to be an ever more important source of growth and job creation. New technology also has the potential to find solutions to pressing economic and social problems. AIM is seen as critical to expediting the entrepreneurial process in India.

7.5.3 Self-Employment and Talent Utilisation (SETU): The National Policy for Skill Development and Entrepreneurs envisaged fostering entrepreneurship and grassroots innovation by providing support in terms of fiscal incentives, creation of grassroots technology innovation hubs, legal support and market linkages. The Government has established a mechanism to be known as SETU under NITI Aayog to support all aspects of start-up businesses and other self-employment activities, particularly in technology-driven areas.

As stated in the Budget Speech of the Finance Minister, 2015-16, SETU is to be a Techno-Financial, Incubation and Facilitation Programme to support all aspects of start-up businesses and other self-employment activities, particularly in technology-driven areas. Initially, a sum of ₹ 1,000 crore was set aside for the purpose

NITI Aayog constituted an Expert Committee on Innovation

and Entrepreneurship (Chairman: Tarun Khanna) in April 2015 for working out the detailed contours of the Atal Innovation Mission (AIM) and SETU to achieve the stated objectives. The Committee submitted its report in August 2015.

7.5.4 Micro Units Development and Refinance Agency (MUDRA): MUDRA is a non-banking financial company (NBFC) which suppors development of micro enterprise sector in India. It provides refinance support to banks/micro finance institutions (MFIs) for lending to micro units having loan requirement up to ₹ 10 lakh. MUDRA provides refinance to micro business under Pradhan Mantri MUDRA Yojana. The other products of MUDRA are meant for development support to the micro enterprise sector.

The services offered by MUDRA—targeted across the spectrum of beneficiary segments—can be categorized as below:

1. Technology enabler.
2. Refinance for micro units to commercial banks, non-banking financial companies (NBFCs), regional rural banks (RRBs), co-operative banks and micro finance institutions (MFIs).

- Shishu: up to ₹ 50,000.
- Kishor: above ₹ 50,000 and up to ₹ 5 lakh.
- Tarun: above ₹ 5 lakh and up to ₹ 10 lakh.

3. Credit guarantee to MUDRA loans.
4. Development and promotional support.

- Sectoral development.
- Skill development.
- Entrepreneurship development.
- Financial literacy.
- Institution development.

7.5.5 Pradhan Mantri MUDRA Yojana (PMMY): Under the aegis of PMMY, MUDRA has created products and schemes. The interventions have been named *Shishu*, *Kishor* and *Tarun* to signify the stage of growth/development and funding needs of the beneficiary micro unit/entrepreneur and also to provide a reference point for the next phase of graduation/growth to look forward to:

1. Shishu: covering loans up to ₹ 50,000
2. Kishor: covering loans above ₹ 50,000 and up to ₹ 5 lakh.
3. Tarun: covering loans above ₹ 5 lakh and up to ₹ 10 lakh.

It is ensured that more focus is given to Shishu category units and then to Kishor and Tarun categories.

Within the framework and overall objective of development and growth of micro enterprises sector under Shishu, Kishor and Tarun, the products being offered by MUDRA are so designed as to meet the requirements of different sectors/business activities as well as business and entrepreneur segments.

Traditional financing in Indian context adopts an asset-based lending approach with emphasis on collaterals. Micro units, most of the times, are unable to provide the comfort of collaterals. Hence MUDRA loans, i.e. loans up to ₹ 10 lakh, have been made collateral free, as per the Reserve Bank of India (RBI) norms in this regard.

To mitigate the issue of collaterals, MUDRA offers a credit guarantee product. MUDRA credit guarantee is extended by creation of a fund called Credit Guarantee Fund for Micro Units (CGFMU) and the scheme was notified by Government of India on April 18, 2016. Accordingly, all eligible micro loans sanctioned since April 8, 2015 are covered under the scheme. The scheme is being managed by National Credit Guarantee Trustee Company (NCGTC), an agency promoted by the Government of India.

Since the individual loan sizes are small and number of loans large, MUDRA credit guarantee scheme provides a portfolio guarantee. Under this, credit guarantee or risk sharing is provided for a portfolio of homogenous loans instead of a scheme for individual loan-by-loan guarantee. This is expected to create administrative efficiencies and increase receptiveness for the credit guarantee product. The guarantee product is one of the key interventions proposed with the objective of bringing down the cost of funds for the end beneficiary to improve its creditworthiness.

The corpus for the credit guarantee scheme is regularly augmented with a charge on the outstanding loans under refinance. The same is utilized for providing first loss guarantee/credit enhancement for securitized portfolio loans.

The funding support from MUDRA is of four types:

1. Micro Credit Scheme (MCS).
2. Refinance Scheme.
3. Women Enterprise Programme.
4. Securitization of Loan Portfolio.

Endnote

1. The report of the Prime Minister's Group—constituted to look into the measures for ensuring growth of the manufacturing sector—submitted in 2008 had recommended the putting in place a well-structured manufacturing sector policy to attain sustained 12-14 percent growth in this sector. The Government released the National Manufacturing Policy (NMP), 2011 on November 4, 2011 for bringing about a quantitative and qualitative change with the following objectives:

- To increase manufacturing sector growth to 12-14 percent over the medium-term.
- To enable manufacturing to contribute at least 25 percent of GDP by 2022.
- To create 100 million additional jobs in the manufacturing sector by 2022.
- To create appropriate skill sets among the rural migrant and urban poor for their easy absorption in manufacturing.
- To increase domestic value addition and technological depth in manufacturing.
- To enhance global competitiveness of Indian manufacturing.

8

Start-up India Initiative

Launched on January 16, 2016, Start-up India is a flagship initiative of the Government of India, intended to build a strong eco-system for nurturing innovation and Start-ups in the country that will drive sustainable economic growth and generate large scale employment opportunities. The Government through this initiative aims to empower Start-ups to grow through innovation and design.

8.1 Meaning of a Start-up

Start-up means an entity, incorporated or registered in India not prior to 5 years, with annual turnover not exceeding ₹ 25 crore in any preceding financial year, working towards innovation, development, deployment or commercialization of new products, processes or services driven by technology or intellectual property.

- Provided that such entity is not formed by splitting up, or reconstruction, of a business already in existence.
- Provided also that an entity shall cease to be a Start-up if its turnover for the previous financial years has exceeded ₹ 25 crore or it has completed 5 years from the date of incorporation/registration.
- Provided further that a Start-up shall be eligible for tax benefits only after it has obtained certification from the Inter-Ministerial Board, setup for such purpose.

8.2 Start-up India: Features

In order to meet the objectives of the initiative, Government of India announced this Action Plan that addresses all aspects of the Start-up ecosystem. With this Action Plan the Government hopes to accelerate spreading of the Start-up movement:

1. From digital/technology sector to a wide array of sectors including agriculture, manufacturing, social sector, healthcare, education, etc.
2. From existing tier 1 cities to tier 2 and tier 3 cities including semi-urban and rural areas.

The action plan is divided across the following areas:

1. Simplification and handholding.
2. Funding support and incentives.
3. Industry-Academia partnership and incubation.

8.3 Simplification and Handholding

8.3.1 Compliance Regime Based on Self-certification: The objective is to reduce the regulatory burden on start-ups thereby allowing them to focus on their core business and keep compliance cost low. Regulatory formalities requiring compliance with various labour and environment laws are time consuming and difficult in nature. Often, new and small firms are unaware of nuances of the issues and can be subjected to intrusive action by regulatory agencies. In order to make compliance for start-ups friendly and flexible, simplifications are required in the regulatory regime.

Accordingly, the process of conducting inspections shall be made more meaningful and simple. Start-ups shall be allowed to self-certify compliance (through the Start-up mobile app) with 9 labour and environment laws. In case of the labour laws, no inspections will be conducted for a period of 3 years. Start-ups may be inspected on receipt of credible and verifiable complaint of violation, filed in writing and approved by at least one level senior to the inspecting officer.

In case of environment laws, start-ups which fall under the *white category* (as defined by the Central Pollution Control Board (CPCB) would be able to self-certify compliance and only random checks would be carried out in such cases.

A. Labour Laws:

1. Building and Other Constructions Workers' (Regulation of

Employment and Conditions of Service) Act, 1996.

2. Inter-State Migrant Workmen (Regulation of Employment and Conditions of Service) Act, 1979.
3. Payment of Gratuity Act, 1972.
4. Contract Labour (Regulation and Abolition) Act, 1970.
5. Employees' Provident Funds and Miscellaneous Provisions Act, 1952.
6. Employees' State Insurance Act, 1948.

B. Environment Laws:

1. Water (Prevention and Control of Pollution) Act, 1974.
2. Water (Prevention and Control of Pollution) Cess (Amendment) Act, 2003.
3. Air (Prevention and Control of Pollution) Act, 1981.

8.3.2 Start-up India HUB: The purpose is to create a single point of contact for the entire Start-up ecosystem and enable knowledge exchange and access to funding. Young Indians today have the conviction to venture out on their own and a conducive ecosystem lets them watch their ideas come to life. In today's environment we have more start-ups and entrepreneurs than ever before and the movement is at the cusp of a revolution. However, many start-ups do not reach their full potential due to limited guidance and access.

The Government of India has taken various measures to improve the ease of doing business and is also building an exciting and enabling environment for these start-ups, with the launch of the "Start-up India" movement.

The "Start-up India Hub" will be a key stakeholder in this vibrant ecosystem and will:

1. Work in a hub and spoke model and collaborate with Central and State governments, Indian and foreign VCs, angel networks, banks, incubators, legal partners, consultants, universities and R&D institutions.
2. Assist start-ups through their lifecycle with specific focus on important aspects like obtaining financing, feasibility testing, business structuring advisory, enhancement of marketing skills, technology commercialization and

management evaluation.

3. Organize mentorship programs in collaboration with government organizations, incubation centres, educational institutions and private organizations who aspire to foster innovation.

To all young Indians who have the courage to enter an environment of risk, the Start-up India Hub will be their friend, mentor and guide to hold their hand and walk with them through this journey.

8.3.3 Rolling-out of Mobile App and Portal: The objective is to serve as the single platform for start-ups for interacting with Government and regulatory institutions for all business needs and information exchange among various stakeholders. In order to commence operations, start-ups require registration with relevant regulatory authorities. Delays or lack of clarity in registration process may lead to delays in establishment and operations of start-ups, thereby reducing the ability of the business to get bank loans, employ workers and generate incomes. Enabling registration process in an easy and timely manner can reduce this burden significantly.

Besides, start-ups often suffer from the uncertainty regarding the exact regulatory requirements to set up its operations. In order to ensure that such information is readily available, it is intended that a checklist of required licenses covering labour licensing, environmental clearances etc. be made available. Currently, the start-up ecosystem in India also lacks formal platform(s) for start-ups to connect and collaborate with other ecosystem partners.

Towards these efforts, the Government shall introduce a mobile app to provide on-the-go accessibility for:

1. Registering start-ups with relevant agencies of the Government. A simple form shall be made available for the same. The mobile app shall have backend integration with Ministry of Corporate Affairs and Registrar of Firms for seamless information exchange and processing of the registration application.

2. Tracking the status of the registration application and anytime downloading of the registration certificate. A digital version of the final registration certificate shall be made available for downloading through the mobile app.
3. Filing for compliances and obtaining information on various clearances/approvals/registrations required.
4. Collaborating with various start-up ecosystem partners. The app shall provide a collaborative platform with a national network of stakeholders (including venture funds, incubators, academia, mentors etc.) of the start-up ecosystem to have discussions towards enhancing and bolstering the ecosystem.
5. Applying for various schemes being undertaken under the Start-up India Action Plan.

The app shall be made available from April 1, 2016 on all leading mobile/smart devices' platforms. The start-up portal shall have similar functionalities (being offered through the mobile app) using a richer web-based user interface.

8.3.4 Legal Support and Fast-tracking Patent Examination at Lower Costs: The objective is to promote awareness and adoption of IPRs by start-ups and facilitate them in protecting and commercializing the IPRs by providing access to high quality intellectual property services and resources, including fast-track examination of patent applications and rebate in fees. Intellectual property rights (IPRs) are emerging as a strategic business tool for any business organization to enhance industrial competitiveness. Start-ups with limited resources and manpower, can sustain in this highly competitive world only through continuous growth and development oriented innovations; for this, it is equally crucial that they protect their IPRs. The scheme for Start-up Intellectual Property Protection (SIPP) shall facilitate filing of patents, trademarks and designs by innovative start-ups. Various measures being taken in this regard include:

1. Fast-tracking of start-up patent applications: The valuation of any innovation goes up immensely, once it gets the protective

cover of a patent. To this end, the patent application of start-ups shall be fast-tracked for examination and disposal, so that they can realize the value of their IPRs at the earliest possible.

2. Panel of facilitators to assist in filing of IP applications: For effective implementation of the scheme, a panel of "facilitators" shall be empanelled by the Controller General of Patents, Designs and Trademarks (CGPDTM), who shall also regulate their conduct and functions. Facilitators will be responsible for providing general advisory on different IPRs as also information on protecting and promoting IPRs in other countries. They shall also provide assistance in filing and disposal of the IP applications related to patents, trademarks and designs under relevant Acts, including appearing on behalf of Start-ups at hearings and contesting opposition, if any, by other parties, till final disposal of the IPR application.
3. Government to bear facilitation cost: Under this scheme, the Central Government shall bear the entire fees of the facilitators for any number of patents, trademarks or designs that a start-up may file, and the start-ups shall bear the cost of only the statutory fees payable.
4. Rebate on filing of application: Start-ups shall be provided an 80 percent rebate in filing of patents vis-à-vis other companies. This will help them pare costs in the crucial formative years.

The scheme is being launched initially on a pilot basis for 1 year; based on the experience gained, further steps shall be taken.

8.3.5 Relaxed Norms of Public Procurement for Start-ups: It is meant to provide an equal platform to start-ups (in the manufacturing sector) vis-à-vis the experienced entrepreneurs in public procurement. Typically, whenever a tender is floated by a Government entity or by a PSU, very often the eligibility condition specifies either "prior experience" or "prior turnover". Such a stipulation prohibits start-ups from participating in such tenders.

At present, effective April 1, 2015, Central Government,

State Government and PSUs have to mandatorily procure at least 20 percent from the micro small and medium enterprises (MSMEs).

In order to promote start-ups, Government shall exempt start-ups (in the manufacturing sector) from the criteria of "prior experience/turnover" without any relaxation in quality standards or technical parameters. The start-ups will also have to demonstrate requisite capability to execute the project as per the requirements and should have their own manufacturing facility in India.

8.3.6 Faster Exit for Start-ups: Given the innovative nature of start-ups, a significant percentage fail to succeed. In the event of a business failure, it is critical to reallocate capital and resources to more productive avenues and accordingly a swift and simple process has been proposed for start-ups to wind-up operations. This will promote entrepreneurs to experiment with new and innovative ideas, without having the fear of facing a complex and long-drawn exit process where their capital remain interminably stuck.

The Insolvency and Bankruptcy Bill 2015 (IBB), tabled in the Lok Sabha in December 2015 has provisions for the fast track and/or voluntary closure of businesses.

In terms of the IBB, start-ups with simple debt structures or those meeting such criteria as may be specified may be wound up within a period of 90 days from making of an application for winding up on a fast track basis.

In such instances, an insolvency professional shall be appointed for the start-up, who shall be in charge of the company (the promoters and management shall no longer run the company) for liquidating its assets and paying its creditors within six months of such appointment. On appointment of the insolvency professional, the liquidator shall be responsible for the swift closure of the business, sale of assets and repayment of creditors in accordance with the distribution waterfall set out in the IBB. This process will respect the concept of limited liability.

8.4 Funding Support and Incentives

8.4.1 Providing Funding Support through a Fund of Funds with a Corpus of ₹ 10,000 crore: One of key challenges faced by start-ups in India has been access to finance. Often start-ups, due to lack of collaterals or existing cash flows, fail to justify the loans. Besides, the high risk nature of start-ups wherein a significant percentage fails to take-off, hampers their investment attractiveness.

In order to provide funding support to start-ups, Government will set up a fund with an initial corpus of ₹ 2,500 crore and a total corpus of ₹ 10,000 crore over a period 4 years (i.e. ₹ 2,500 crore per year). The Fund will be in the nature of Fund of Funds, which means that it will not invest directly into start-ups, but shall participate in the capital of SEBI registered venture funds.

Key features of the Fund of Funds are highlighted below:

1. The Fund of Funds shall be managed by a Board with private professionals drawn from industry bodies, academia, and successful start-ups.
2. Life Insurance Corporation (LIC) shall be a co-investor in the Fund of Funds.
3. The Fund of Funds shall contribute to a maximum of 50 percent of the stated daughter fund size. In order to be able to receive the contribution, the daughter fund should have already raised the balance 50 percent or more of the stated fund size as the case maybe. The Fund of Funds shall have representation on the governance structure/board of the venture fund based on the contribution made.
4. The Fund shall ensure support to a broad mix of sectors such as manufacturing, agriculture, health, education, etc.

8.4.2 Credit Guarantee Fund for Start-ups: In order to overcome traditional Indian stigma associated with failure of start-up enterprises in general and to encourage experimentation among start-up entrepreneurs through disruptive business models, credit guarantee comfort would help flow of venture debt from the formal banking system.

Debt funding to start-ups is also perceived as high risk area and to encourage banks and other lenders to provide venture debts to start-ups, credit guarantee mechanism through National Credit Guarantee Trust Company (NCGTC)/SIDBI is being envisaged with a budgetary corpus of ₹ 500 crore per year for the next four years.

8.4.3 Tax Exemption on Capital Gains: Due to their high risk nature, start-ups are not able to attract investment in their initial stage. It is therefore important that suitable incentives are provided to investors for investing in the start-up ecosystem. With this objective, exemption shall be given to persons who have capital gains during the year, if they have invested such capital gains in the Fund of Funds recognized by the Government.

This will augment the funds available to various VCs for investment in start-ups.

In addition, existing capital gain tax exemption for investment in newly formed manufacturing MSMEs by individuals shall be extended to all start-ups. Currently, such an entity needs to purchase "new assests" with the capital gain received to avail such an exemption. Investment in 'computer or computer software' (as used in core business activity) shall also be considered as purchase of 'new assets' in order to promote technology driven start-ups.

8.4.4 Tax Exemption to Start-ups for 3 years: Innovation is the essence of every start-up. Young minds kindle new ideas every day to think beyond conventional strategies of the existing corporate world.

During the initial years, budding entrepreneurs struggle to evaluate the feasibility of their business idea. Significant capital investment is made in embracing ever-changing technology, fighting rising competition and navigating through the unique challenges arising from their venture. Also, there are limited alternative sources of finance available to the small and growing entrepreneurs, leading to constrained cash funds.

With a view to stimulate the development of start-ups in

India and provide them a competitive platform, it is imperative that the profits of start-up initiatives are exempted from income-tax for a period of 3 years. This fiscal exemption shall facilitate growth of business and meet the working capital requirements during the initial years of operations. The exemption shall be available subject to non-distribution of dividend by the start-up.

8.4.5 Tax Exemption on Investments above Fair Market Value: Under The Income Tax Act, 1961, where a start-up (company) receives any consideration for issue of shares which exceeds the fair market value (FMV) of such shares, such excess consideration is taxable in the hands of recipient as income from other sources.

In the context of start-ups, where the idea is at a conceptualization or development stage, it is often difficult to determine the FMV of such shares. In majority of the cases, FMV is also significantly lower than the value at which the capital investment is made. This results into the tax being levied under Section 56 (2) (viib).

Currently, investment by venture capital funds in start-ups is exempted from operations of this provision. The same shall be extended to investment made by incubators in the start-ups.

8.5 Industry-Academia Partnership and Incubation

8.5.1 Organizing Start-up Fests for Showcasing Innovation and Providing a Collaboration Platform: A pivotal component for growth of start-ups is regular communication and collaboration within the start-up community, both national as well international. An effective start-up ecosystem cannot be created by the start-ups alone. It is dependent on active participation of academia, investors, industry and other stakeholders.

To bolster the start-up ecosystem in India, the Government is proposing to introduce start-up fests at national and international stages.

These fests would provide a platform to start-ups in India to showcase their ideas and work with a larger audience comprising of potential investors, mentors and fellow start-ups.

As part of Make in India initiative, Government proposes to:

1. Hold one fest at the national level annually to enable all the stakeholders of start-up ecosystem to come together on one platform.
2. Hold one fest at the international level annually in an international city known for its start-up ecosystem.

The fests shall have activities such as sessions to connect with investors, mentors, incubators and start-ups, showcasing innovations, exhibitions and product launches, pitches by start-ups, mentoring sessions, curated start-up walks, talks by disruptive innovators, competitions such as Hackathon, Makerspace, etc., announcements of rewards and recognitions, panels and conferences with industry leaders etc.

8.5.2 Launch of Atal Innovation Mission (AIM) with Self-Employment and Talent Utilization (SETU) Programme: The objective is to serve as a platform for promotion of world-class Innovation hubs, grand challenges, start-up businesses and other self-employment activities, particularly in technology driven areas. The Atal Innovation Mission (AIM) shall have two core functions:

1. Entrepreneurship promotion through Self-Employment and Talent Utilization (SETU), wherein innovators would be supported and mentored to become successful entrepreneurs.
2. Innovation promotion: to provide a platform where innovative ideas are generated.

The main components proposed to be undertaken as part of the mission include:

A. Entrepreneurship Promotion:

1. Establishment of sector specific Incubators including in PPP mode.
2. Establishment of 500 tinkering labs.
3. Pre-incubation training to potential entrepreneurs in various technology areas in collaboration with various academic institutions having expertise in the field.

4. Strengthening of incubation facilities in existing incubators and mentoring of start-ups.
5. Seed funding to potentially successful and high growth start-ups.

B. Innovation Promotion:

1. Institution of innovation awards (3 per state/UT) and 3 National level awards.
2. Providing support to State Innovation Councils for awareness creation and organizing state level workshops/conferences.
3. Launch of Grand Innovation Challenge Awards for finding ultra-low cost solutions to India's pressing and intractable problems.

8.5.3 Harnessing Private Sector Expertise for Incubator Setup: This is meant to ensure professional management of Government sponsored/funded incubators, Government will create a policy and framework for setting-up of incubators across the country in public private partnership. India currently lacks availability of incubation facilities across various parts of the country. Incubation facilities typically include physical infrastructure, provision of mentorship support, access to networks, access to market, etc. Of all these features, physical infrastructure entails large capital investments which can generally be facilitated by the Government. However, requisite skills for operating an incubator are pivotal as well, for which expertise of the private sector needs to be leveraged. Considering this, Government shall encourage setting up of

1. 35 new incubators in existing institutions. Funding support of 40 percent (subject to a maximum of ₹ 10 crore) shall be provided by Central Government for establishment of new incubators for which 40 percent funding by the respective State Government and 20 percent funding by the private sector has been committed. The incubator shall be managed and operated by the private sector.
2. 35 new private sector incubators. A grant of 50 percent (subject to a maximum of ₹ 10 crore) shall be provided by Central Government for incubators established by

private sector in existing institutions. The incubator shall be managed and operated by the private sector.

The funding for setting up of the incubators shall be provided by NITI Aayog as part of Atal Innovation Mission. Participating departments and agencies for setting up of new incubators shall be Department of Science and Technology, Department of Biotechnology, Department of Electronics and Information Technology, Ministry of Micro, Small and Medium Enterprises, Department of Higher Education, Department of Industrial Policy and Promotion and NITI Aayog.

Each of the above mentioned departments/agencies would enter into a standard MoU with identified private sector players for creation of academia-industry tie-ups for nurturing innovations in academic institutions.

8.5.4 Building Innovation Centres at National Institutes: In order to augment the incubation and R&D efforts in the country, the Government will set up/scale up 31 centres (to provide facilities for over 1,200 new start-ups) of innovation and entrepreneurship at national institutes, including:

1. Setting-up 13 Start-up centres: Annual funding support of ₹ 50 lakh (shared 50:50 by DST and MHRD) shall be provided for three years for encouraging student driven Start-ups from the host institute.
2. Setting-up/Scaling-up 18 Technology Business Incubators (TBIs) at NITs/IITs/IIMs etc. as per funding model of DST with MHRD providing smooth approvals for TBI to have separate society and built up space.

8.5.5 Setting up of 7 New Research Parks Modelled on the Research Park Setup at IIT Madras: The Government shall set up 7 new research parks in institutes indicated below with an initial investment of ₹ 100 crore each. The research parks shall be modelled based on the research park setup at IIT Madras.

IIT Madras Research Park endeavours to enable companies with a research focus to set up a base in the Park and leverage the expertise of IIT Madras. The Research Park breaks down the traditional, artificial barriers of innovation through its connectivity and collaborative interaction. This helps industry to create, integrate and apply advancements in knowledge. It leverages best practices from successful research parks such as those at Stanford, MIT and Cambridge.

The guiding principles behind the park include:

1. Creating a collaborative environment between industry and academia through joint research projects and consulting assignments.
2. Creating a self-sustaining and technologically fertile environment.
3. Encouraging and enabling R&D activities and start-ups that are aligned to potential needs of the industry.
4. Providing world class infrastructure for R&D activities and incubation.
5. Enabling development of high quality personnel and motivating professional growth for researchers in companies through part-time Masters' and Ph.D. programmes.

8.5.6 Promoting Start-ups in the Biotechnology Sector: The Biotechnology sector in India is on a strong, growth trajectory. Department of Biotechnology endeavours to scale up the number of Start-ups in the sector by nurturing approximately 300-500 new start-ups each year to have around 2,000 start-ups by 2020. In order to promote start-ups in the sector, The Department of Biotechnology shall be implementing the following measures along with its Public Sector Undertaking Biotechnology Research Assistance Council (BIRAC):

A. Bio-incubators, Seed Fund and Equity Funding:

1. 5 new bio-clusters, 50 new bio-Incubators, 150 technology transfer offices and 20 bio-connect offices will be set up in research institutes and universities across India.
2. Biotech Equity Fund—BIRAC AcE Fund in partnership with National and Global Equity Funds (Bharat Fund, India Aspiration Fund amongst others) will provide financial assistance to young biotech start-ups.

B. Encouraging and Leveraging Global Partnerships:

1. Bengaluru-Boston Biotech Gateway to India has been formed. Letter of intent has been signed between DBT, Government of India and Department of IT, Government of Karnataka for the same. Through this initiative, a range of institutes in Boston (Harvard/MIT) and Bengaluru will be able to connect to share ideas and mentor the entrepreneurs especially in the areas of genomics, computational biology, drug discovery and new vaccines.
2. Amplification of Bio-entrepreneurship through BIRAC Regional Entrepreneurship Centres (BREC). The BREC aims to impart bio-entrepreneurs with the necessary knowledge and skills required for converting innovative ideas into successful ventures. Department of Biotechnology shall set up 5 regional centres or mini-BIRACs in the next 5 years.

8.5.7 Launching of Innovation Focused Programs for Students: In order to promote research and innovation among young students, the Government shall implement the following measures:

1. **Innovation Core:** Innovation Core programme shall be initiated to target school kids with an outreach to 10 lakh innovations from 5 lakh schools. One lakh innovations would be targeted and the top 10,000 innovations would be provided prototyping support. Of these 10,000 innovations, the best 100 would be short listed and showcased at the Annual Festival of Innovations in the Rashtrapati Bhavan.
2. **NIDHI:** A Grand Challenge program (National Initiative for Developing and Harnessing Innovations) shall be instituted through Innovation and Entrepreneurship Development Centres (IEDCs) to support and award ₹ 10 lakh to 20 student innovations from IEDCs.
3. **Uchhattar Avishkar Yojana:** A joint MHRD-DST scheme which has earmarked ₹ 250 crore per annum towards fostering "very high quality" research amongst IIT students. The funding towards this research will be 50

percent contribution from MHRD, 25 percent from DST and 25 percent from industry. This format has been devised to ensure that the research and funding gets utilized bearing in mind its relevance to the industry. Each project may amount to ₹ 5 crore only. This scheme will initially apply to IITs only.

8.5.8 Annual Incubator Grand Challenge: For a new idea to become a successful commercial venture, adequate support and mentoring at various stages of the business lifecycle is required. Incubators play an important role in identifying early stage start-ups and supporting them across various phases of their lifecycle. In order to build an effective start-up ecosystem, it is imperative that world class incubators, adopting leading industry practices, are setup in the country.

The Government is proposing to make forward looking investments towards building world class incubators. In its first phase, the aim is to establish 10 such incubators. To enable this, Government of India shall identify and select 10 incubators who have the potential to become world class. These incubators would be given ₹ 10 crore each as financial assistance which may be used for ramping up the quality of service offerings. The incubators shall also become reference models for other incubators aspiring to offer best-in-class services. Video interviews of these incubators would be showcased on the Start-up India portal.

An "Incubator Grand Challenge" exercise shall be carried out for identification of these incubators. The exercise shall entail:

1. Open invitation of applications from incubators.
2. Screening and evaluation based on pre-defined key performance indicators (KPIs).

The Incubator Grand Challenge shall be an annual exercise.

8.6 India Aspiration Fund (IAF) for Start-ups

IAF is aimed to catalyse tens of thousands of crores of equity investment into start-ups and micro, small and medium enterprises (MSMEs) creating employment of lakhs of persons, mostly educated youth, over the next four to five years.

For details, see section 4.2 of chapter 4 of this book.

9

Stand-up India Scheme

Scheduled castes (SCs) and scheduled tribes (STs) entrepreneurs are beginning to show great promise in starting and running successful business enterprises. The Prime Minister had given a call for promoting entrepreneurship among SCs/STs to become job providers rather than job seekers.

In the above context, the Finance Minister in his Budget Speech for the year 2016-17 remarked, "We are celebrating the 125th Birth Anniversary of Dr. B.R. Ambedkar. This must become the Year of Economic Empowerment for SC/ST entrepreneurs. We have extensively interacted with the Dalit India Chamber of Commerce and Industry on building an entrepreneurship ecosystem. It is proposed to constitute a National Scheduled Caste and Scheduled Tribe Hub in the MSME Ministry in partnership with industry associations. This Hub will provide professional support to scheduled caste and scheduled tribe entrepreneurs to fulfil the obligations under the Central Government procurement policy 2012, adopt global best practices and leverage the Stand-Up India initiative". [1]

9.1 Main Features of Stand-up India Scheme

The Start-up India and Stand-up India initiatives were announced by Prime Minister Shri Narendra Modi in his address to the nation from the ramparts of Red Fort on August 15, 2015. Thereafter, the Union Cabinet approved the Stand up India Scheme in January 2016. Government of India launched the Stand-up India scheme on April 5, 2016.

The scheme facilitates bank loans between ₹ 10 lakh and ₹ 1 crore to at least one scheduled caste (SC)/scheduled tribe (ST) borrower and at least one woman borrower per bank branch for setting up greenfield enterprises. This enterprise may be in manufacturing, services or the trading sector. The scheme which is being implemented through all scheduled commercial banks is to benefit at least 2.5 lakh borrowers. The scheme is operational and the loan is being extended through scheduled commercial banks across the country.

Stand-up India scheme caters to promoting entrepreneurship amongst women, SCs and STs categories, i.e. those sections of the population facing significant hurdles due to lack of advice/mentorship as well as inadequate and delayed credit. The scheme intends to leverage the institutional credit structure to reach out to these underserved sectors of the population in starting greenfield enterprises. It caters to both ready and trainee borrowers.

Some of the features of this scheme are as under:

1. The Stand up India scheme is anchored by Department of Financial Services (DFS), Ministry of Finance to encourage greenfield enterprises by scheduled castes (SCs)/scheduled tribes (STs) and women entrepreneurs.
2. The scheme is intended to facilitate at least two such projects per bank branch, on an average, one for each category of entrepreneur.
3. The expected date of reaching the target of at least 2.5 lakh approvals is 36 months from the launch of the scheme.
4. The scheme provides for refinance window through Small Industries Development Bank of India (SIDBI) with an initial amount of ₹ 10,000 crore.
5. The scheme provides for creation of a credit guarantee mechanism through the National Credit Guarantee Trustee Company (NCGTC).
6. The scheme provides for handholding support for borrowers both at the pre-loan stage and during operations. This would include increasing their familiarity with factoring services, registration with online platforms and e-market places as well as sessions on best practices and problem solving.
7. The scheme focuses on handholding support for both

SCs/STs and women borrowers.

8. The scheme's overall intent is to leverage the institutional credit structure to reach out to these under-served sectors of the population by facilitating bank loans repayable up to 7 years and between ₹ 10 lakh to ₹ 100 lakh for greenfield enterprises in the non-farm sector set up by such SCs, STs and women borrowers.
9. The loan under the scheme would be appropriately secured and backed by a credit guarantee through a credit guarantee scheme for which Department of Financial Services would be the settler and National Credit Guarantee Trustee Company Ltd. (NCGTC) would be the operating agency.
10. Margin money of the composite loan under the scheme would be up to 25 percent. Convergence with state schemes is expected to reduce the actual requirement of margin money for a number of borrowers. Over a period of time, it is proposed that a credit history of the borrower be built-up through credit bureaus.

As on March 29, 2017, ₹ 5,237.29 crore had been sanctioned in 25,435 accounts—women (20,305), SCs (4,044) and STs (1,086).

9.2 Dalit Indian Chamber of Commerce and Industry (DICCI)

Pune-based DICCI was established in 2005 by Milind Kamble, a civil engineer and entrepreneur. The organization has grown with the help of 18 State Chapters and 7 International Chapters. Its membership base is rapidly expanding as more dalit entrepreneurs become aware of its activities and what it can offer them.

The activities of its members are quite diversified ranging from manufacturing (sectors such as chemicals, agri-products, frozen foods, plastics, textiles, pest control, metals and metallurgy, marine engineering, solar energy, sugar refining), construction and services (health care, hospitality industries, education and international trade).

DICCI's tag lines explain its philosophy:

Be job givers—not job seekers.

Fight caste with capital.

DICCI operates with a three-fold mandate:

- Bring together all dalit entrepreneurs under one umbrella.
- Become a one-stop resource centre for existing and aspiring dalit entrepreneurs.
- Promote entrepreneurship among dalits as a solution to their socio-economic problems.

DICCI has the mission to motivate dalit youth to enter business and industry as entrepreneurs and to carve their own niche. It aims to encourage them to contribute to the nation's economy through wealth creation and to spread the spirit of enterprise to other fellow members.

DICCI is treading the path of learning and enrichment through networking and knowledge exchange by following means:

- Business trade fairs.
- Seminars and workshops.
- Interaction with industry and Government.
- Share the information on latest trends and opportunities.

9.2.1 Challenges for DICCI: It faces many challenges in terms of fostering entrepreneurship among the community:

1. Availability of early-stage funding.
2. Creating professional entrepreneurship development programmes (EDPs) tailored for their needs without ignoring their social setting.
3. Helping existing dalit entrepreneurs scale-up their operations and grow.

Endnote

1. Government of India, Ministry of Finance, *Speech of the Finance Minister, 2016-17*, para 57.

10

Mahatma Gandhi National Rural Employment Guarantee Act (MGNREGA), 2005

MGNREGA was notified on September 7, 2005. The Act came into force on February 2, 2006 when 200 selected districts of the country were brought under its purview (Phase I, 2006-07). MGNREGA was extended to additional 130 districts in Phase II during 2007-08. The remaining rural areas were notified with effect from April 1, 2008.

10.1 Objectives and Significance of MGNREGA

The objective of the MGNREGA is to enhance the livelihood security of unorganised workers in rural areas by guaranteeing 100 days of wage employment in a financial year to a rural household whose members volunteer to do unskilled manual work. The Act further aims at creating durable assets and strengthening the livelihood resource base of the rural poor. The choice of works suggested in the Act address causes of chronic poverty like drought, deforestation, soil erosion, etc. so that the process of employment generation is on a sustainable basis.

The significance of MGNREGA lies in the fact that it creates a right-based framework for wage employment programmes and makes the Government legally bound to provide employment to those who seek it. In this way the legislation goes beyond providing a social safety net, and towards guaranteeing the right to employment. By prioritizing natural resource management and emphasizing the creation of durable assets it holds the potential of becoming a growth engine for sustainable development of an agriculture-based economy.

Under MGNREGA, employment is dependent upon the

worker exercising the choice to apply for registration, obtain a job card and then to seek employment through a written application for the time and duration chosen by her. The legal guarantee has to be fulfilled within the time limit prescribed and this mandate is underpinned by the provision of unemployment allowance. The Act is thus designed to offer an incentive structure to the States for providing employment as ninety percent of the cost for employment provided is borne by the Centre, and there is a concomitant disincentive for not providing employment, if demanded, as the States then bear the double indemnity of unemployment and the cost of unemployment allowance.

Earlier wage employment programmes were allocation based. However, MGNREGA is not supply driven but demand driven. Resource transfer under MGNREGA is based on the demand for employment and this provides another critical incentive to States to leverage the Act to meet the employment needs of the poor. The delivery system has been made accountable, as it envisages an Annual Report on the outcomes of MGNREGA to be presented by the Central Government to the Parliament and to the State Legislature by the State Government.

10.2 Funding of the Programme

The Central Government bears the costs on the following items:

1. The entire cost of wages of unskilled manual workers.
2. 75 percent of the cost of material, wages of skilled and semi skilled workers.
3. Administrative expenses as may be determined by the Central Government, which will include inter alia, the salary and the allowances of the Programme Officer and his supporting staff, work site facilities.
4. Expenses of the National Employment Guarantee Council.

The State Government bears the costs on the following items:

1. 25 percent of the cost of material, wages of skilled and

semi skilled workers (As a ratio of 60:40 is to be maintained for wages of the unskilled manual workers and the material, skilled/semi skilled workers' wages, the State Government has to bear only 25 percent of the 40 percent component, which means a contribution of 10 percent of the expenditure).

2. Unemployment allowance payable in case the State Government cannot provide wage employment on time.
3. Administrative expenses of the State Employment Guarantee Council.

10.3 Expression of Demand for Employment

Since MGNREGA is a right-based programme, expression of demand for employment by the rural poor is the basic premise of its operation, especially if the wage seekers are illiterate and unorganized. Generating awareness about the programme among local rural communities becomes critical for enabling the rural poor to express demand. States have adopted various methods for communication and social mobilisation that include preparation of communication material on MGNREGA processes in simple local language, orientation of sarpanches/ward members, convening gram sabhas, using district teams for village level interactions, local vernacular newspapers, TV and radio spots, pamphlets and brochures, local cultural forums, fixing a Rozgar Day in a week and establishing a helpline. The full knowledge of the rights that MGNREGA confers on the rural poor is the most important pre-requisite to enable them to seek employment as per their choice of time and duration.

10.4 Labour Budget, Inventory of Projects and Perspective Plan

MGNREGA guarantees providing employment within 15 days of demand and the instrument for providing employment is unskilled manual work selected from the list of permissible works. This legal guarantee has implication for the way in which works have to be planned.

A labour budget, as stipulated under the Act, is required to be prepared to facilitate advance planning, whereby districts estimate their labour demand for the ensuing financial year by December end.

National guidelines indicate the way in which the annual shelf of projects may be prepared to meet the estimated labour demand. Districts should keep a list of works ready to meet employment demand. Estimated benefits in terms of person days need to be assessed, so that the employment expected to be generated through the works planned may be clearly matched with the estimated employment demand. Physical improvement envisaged (land/water conservation etc.) has to be quantified so that the focus remains on creating durable and productive assets that support further self-sustaining employment. Displaying the list of approved works at the gram panchayat office and the details of works taken up on the work site has been stipulated so that the workers know the work opportunities locally available.

National guidelines lay down the broad principles of preparing a Five Year District Perspective Plan that must have the following components, viz. village mapping of natural resources and social infrastructure, identification of gaps and works that can be taken up as per MGNREGA permissible list, assessment of works that respond to what local people want, what will build a livelihood base to enable them to move out of MGNREGA to sustainable employment and assessment of labour demand.

10.5 Work Record, Payment of Wages and Preventing Bogus Muster Rolls

The legal guarantee of MGNREGA mandates that wages due to workers be paid within 15 days of work completion. This requires that a fair record be maintained for the work done. To ensure that authentic muster rolls are used, numbered muster rolls are to be issued for each sanctioned work by programme officer and maintained on the work site by the executing agency. Muster rolls must mention job card numbers of workers, days worked, quantum of work done, amount paid and must have space for recording inspections.

Muster rolls should be read out on the work site during measurement and wage payment to prevent bogus records. Entries of the muster roll should be correspondingly recorded in the job cards of the workers. Updating of muster roll data at the block level computers in a 15 days cycle needs to be ensured. Regular measurement and supervision of works should be done by qualified technical personnel on time.

10.6 Vigilance and Transparency

Vigilance and transparency have been strongly emphasized in MGNREGA. The field verification of MGNREGA processes is through external and internal agencies and the feedback is shared with the States for follow up. Independent concurrent studies have also been taken up. Monitoring at the State level is required and States are expected to ensure 100 percent verification at block level, 10 percent at district level and 2 percent at the state level, especially of work muster rolls, and records. Guidelines for muster roll verification have been evolved. The setting up and training local vigilance and monitoring committees is also required for bringing in lateral transparency.

A web-enabled MIS www.nrega.nic.in has been developed that seeks to place all information in public domain. It is a household level database and has internal checks for ensuring consistency and conformity to normative processes. All critical parameters get monitored in public domain.

10.7 Other Processes of MGNREGA

10.7.1 Right-based Framework:

1. Adult members of a rural household who are willing to do unskilled manual work may apply for registration to the local gram panchayat, in writing, or orally.
2. Gram panchayat after due verification will issue a job

card. The job card will bear the photograph of all adult members of the household and is free of cost.

3. A job card holding household may submit a written application for employment to the Gram Panchayat, stating the time and duration for which work is sought.

10.7.2 Women Empowerment: MGNREGA stipulates that priority shall be given to women. In terms of implementation it mandates that a minimum of one-third of the beneficiaries shall be women who have registered and have requested for work.

10.7.3 Public Accountability: MGNREGA contains specific provisions for public accountability. This has to be accomplished through the provisions made in the Act and guidelines regarding right to information, proactive disclosure of information and a transparent social audit process. The right to information should be followed in both letter and spirit in all matters relating to MGNREGA. Section 17 of MGNREGA provides for social audit of all works in a gram panchayat (GP) by the gram sabha and the gram panchayat has to provide records for social audit.

10.7.4 Grievance Redressal: Enforcement of the right to employment requires setting up an effective grievance redressal system. MGNREGA vests the responsibility for grievance redressal with the programme officer. To ensure prompt grievance redressal, certain basic arrangements must be ensured, such as setting up a grievance redressal cell at the programme officer (PO)/district programme co-ordinator (DPC) offices, preferably with a toll free helpline. The PO and DPC must review the disposal of complaints on a monthly basis and the persons concerned must be informed.

10.7.5 Financial Management: A non-lapsable Central Employment Guarantee Fund has been set up to ensure that availability of funds match working season demands. Districts have dedicated accounts for MGNREGA funds and submit their proposals based on clearly delineated guidelines so that funds may be devolved efficiently at each level, and adequate funds may be available to respond to demand. The funds are released on the basis of demand for employment received in a district and are based on an appraisal of both financial and physical indicators of outcomes.

10.7.6 Time-bound Guarantee:

1. Gram panchayat will issue a dated receipt of the written application for employment, against which the guarantee of providing employment within 15 days operates. If employment is not provided within 15 days, daily unemployment allowance in cash has to be paid. Liability of payment of unemployment allowance is of the States.
2. Work should ordinarily be provided within 5 km. radius of the village or else extra wages of 10 percent are payable
3. Wages are to be paid according to minimum wages. Disbursement of wages has to be done on weekly basis and not beyond a fortnight. With wages indexed to the consumer price index for agricultural labour (CPI-AL), the average wage under the scheme has increased from ₹ 65 in 2006-07 to ₹ 132 in 2013-14, resulting in improvement in the bargaining power of agriculture labour. It has also led to improved economic outcomes, especially in watershed activities, and reduction in distress migration.

10.7.7 Work Site Facilities: Work site facilities such as crèche, drinking water, shade have to be provided.

10.7.8 Labour-intensive Works: A 60:40 wage and material ratio has to be maintained. Contractors and use of labour displacing machinery is prohibited.

10.7.9 Permissible Works:

1. Water conservation.
2. Drought proofing (including plantation and afforestation).
3. Irrigation canals.
4. Minor irrigation, horticulture and land development on the lands of scheduled castes, scheduled tribes, and land reform beneficiaries.
5. Renovation of traditional water bodies.
6. Flood protection.

7. Land development.
8. Rural connectivity.
9. Any other work that may be notified by the Central Government in consultation with the State Government.

10.7.10 Rozgar Jagaran Puruskar: The objective of the award is to acknowledge the outstanding and exemplary contribution made by a registered Civil Society Organizations (CSO) in the effective implementation of the MGNREGA at state, district, block and gram panchayat levels. The award includes a medal, scroll and cash (gram panchayat, ₹ 1,000; intermediate panchayat, ₹ 2,000; district panchayat, ₹ 5,000 and State level, ₹ 25,000).

10.8 National Rural Employment Guarantee Act Software Package (NREGASoft)

MoRD and NIC commenced the preparation of appropriate e-governance solution to strengthen NREGA in October 2005 and when the scheme was launched in February 2006, the NREGASoft was also launched across the country. The software is available to all stakeholders online through http://nrega.nic.in and also could be downloaded for off-line working. The package is unicode-enabled and supports local languages. The training to use the software has been organized in States.

NREGAsoft is web-based software prepared to capture all the activities under NREGA at national/state/district/block and panchayat level. Using this portal, each stakeholder can input information and access his/her own information through this portal. NREGAsoft captures Registration of workers, work demanded, number of days of employment for whole family, funds transferred/utilized and number of works undertaken under the scheme. Various stakeholders of the project are the following:

1. Citizens.
2. Gram panchayats, block panchayats zilla panchayats.
3. Workers.

4. Programme officers.
5. District programme co-ordinators.
6. Implementing agencies other then PRIs.
7. State RD Departments.
8. Ministry of Rural Development and administrators in Government of India.

Various modules of the software are the following:

10.8.1 Beneficiary Management Module: It captures registration, demand for work, work allocation and muster rolls on which a person worked, the software has the provision of payment of wages through bank/post office as it captures the bank/post office account number, bank/post office name, branch name for all the person who demanded job and their account number are shown in muster roll against their name and calculate unemployment allowance, if any and also keep tracks of number of days of employment of a family.

10.8.2 Fund Management Module: It captures the funds transferred from MoRD/States to districts and then to programme officers/panchayats and expenditure incurred by various implementing agencies on labour, material and contingency. Hence, it keeps track of each and every paisa spent under the scheme.

10.8.3 Works Management Module: It captures information about the various works undertaken under the scheme at various levels. It facilitates online approval of projects and keeps track of time taken for approval of project. Each project is provided a unique ID and status of work is maintained in the system

10.8.4 Grievance Redressal System: It allows a worker/citizen to lodge complaint and trace the subsequent response.

10.8.5 Staffing Position Module: It captures name, telephone numbers etc. of all the officials, planning and implementing agencies from gram panchayat to MoRD involved in NREGA, thus strengthening communication and coordination among them.

10.8.6 Alerts: The software also gives alerts to implementing agencies about the various irregularities, important activities, messages for funds to be received by the agencies.

10.8.7 Gram Panchayat Accounting System: NREGA put lot of responsibility on gram panchayats as registration, demand for work and allocation of work can be done only by gram panchayats. Software assists gram panchayats as follows:

1. It keeps track of 100 days of the employment to a family.
2. It ensures that a worker should not work on two worksites simultaneously.
3. The software keeps track of the fund released from the MoRD/States to the districts and then from districts to blocks/gram panchayats so it helps in reconciliation of accounts
4. It provides status of available funds in the accounts at panchayats, blocks and districts levels.

10.9 Twelfth Five Year Plan (2012-17) on MGNREGA

Commenting on the performance of MGNREGA, the Approach Paper to the Twelfth Plan observed, "With a people-centred, demand-driven architecture, completely different from the earlier rural employment programmes, MGNREGA has directly led to the creation of 987 crore person-days of work since its inception in 2006-07. In financial year 2010-11, MGNREGA provided employment to 5.45 crore households generating 253.68 crore person-days. It has also successfully raised the negotiating power of agricultural labour, resulting in higher agricultural wages, improved economic outcomes leading to reduction in distress migration. This is not to deny that with better project design, implementation leakages could be greatly reduced; and the assets so created could make a larger contribution towards increase in land productivity.

Reforms in implementation of Plan schemes are a priority and should receive focussed attention in the Twelfth Plan. There is need for more flexibility in the design of the schemes to reflect the ground realities across the States. Additional provisions should be considered for encouraging innovation; also special efforts to promote convergence at the level of implementation to prevent duplication and to create synergies that improve the quality of outcomes". [1]

The Plan Document further stated, "Experience thus far suggests that while MGNREGA is generating employment, the technical soundness of design and quality of works undertaken in MGNREGA falls short of what is needed to ensure land productivity enhancement. There appear to be two critical areas in regard of MGNREGA that need to be addressed and resolved in the Twelfth Plan.

First, the technical capacity at the local level has to be significantly enhanced. This is in regard to planning, design and quality of works, as well as of their maintenance. Planning for MGNREGA on a mini-watershed and aquifer basis would improve outcomes. To strengthen the demand-driven character of the scheme and guarantee legal entitlements, it is important to record applications for work. There is a clear case for establishing a pool of local 'barefoot' engineers/technical assistants who could be trained up through an appropriate mechanism, enabling them to fulfil the need for technical and managerial capacity in MGNREGA, as well as in other rural infrastructure projects

Second, it is important that the selection of works reflects the needs, aspirations and priorities of the local people, without which the community will not necessarily have a sense of ownership of the project. The latter is a vital component of the concept of rural infrastructure creation. The training of a pool of local youth in technical skills must also incorporate their ability to act as social mobilizers and ensure the involvement of panchayati raj institution (PRI) representatives at every level of the process. They would be guided in this process by a dedicated team of technical professionals (to be created) at each cluster of around 30 villages that broadly correspond to the boundaries of a mini-watershed and aquifer. Madhya Pradesh and Maharashtra have already initiated work in this direction.

Delays in wage payments have emerged as the most frequently heard complaint under MGNREGA. At times, payments have not been made even after nine months and workers are rarely being paid compensation for the delay. The major reason for delay is that measurements of work are not being made on time, mainly due to lack of adequate technical staff at the block level. There are also bottlenecks in the flow of funds through the system, at times because data on the management information system (MIS) is not being filled up on time. Better use of information technology, as in Andhra Pradesh, is worth emulating. The tightly integrated, end-to-end computer network in Andhra Pradesh identifies delay in execution of any work registered online and takes corrective action immediately. Free availability of payment information facilitates public scrutiny and transparency.

There is a need to involve NGOs who could support gram panchayats in planning, implementing and conducting of social audits of MGNREGA works. There are good examples of such successful models across the country. There is a need to disseminate the learnings from these experiences in the field and improve the functioning of the programme.

Rural India has a large population of artisan families, many of whom are from the minority and tribal communities. Most of these artisan farmers do not own any land and many find themselves in a difficult condition with poor access to market linkages and to remunerative livelihoods. Thought must be given as to how the MGNREGA in conjunction with the NRLM programme can help these artisan communities to obtain a decent living while at the same time conserving the base of craftsmanship, which is India's cultural heritage". [2]

10.10 Some Recent Initiatives under the Mahatma Gandhi NREGA

- Inter-departmental convergence and collaboration activities like construction of individual household latrines under the

Nirmal Bharat Abhiyan (NBA), construction of anganwadi centres under the Integrated Child Development Services (ICDS) Scheme, construction of village playfields under the Panchayat Yuva Krida aur Khel Abhiyan, and convergence with watershed management programmes.

- Steps to open individual bank/post office accounts for all women workers.
- Identifying and providing job cards to widowed, deserted, and destitute women.
- Initiatives for the disabled and other vulnerable persons by fixing schedule of rates (SoR) based on work and time motion study at state level.
- Adding new works to the existing list of permissible works specifically focused on rural livelihood and agricultural activities.

In short, Mahatma Gandhi NREGA aims at providing not less than 100 days of guaranteed wage employment in a financial year to every rural household, with a stipulation of one-third participation of women, through creation of assets that address causes of chronic poverty like drought, deforestation, and soil erosion, thus encouraging sustainable development.

10.11 New Guidelines to Strengthen Demand-driven Character of MGNREGA

1. The gram panchayat or programme officer, as the case may be, shall be bound to accept valid applications and to issue a dated receipt to the applicant.
2. Refusal to accept applications and provide dated receipts will be treated as a contravention under Section 25 of MGNREGA.
3. The provision for submitting applications for work must be kept available on a continuous basis through multiple channels so designated by gram panchayats who may empower ward members, anganwadi workers, school teachers, self-help groups, village-level revenue functionaries, common service centres and Mahatma Gandhi

NREGA Labour Groups to receive applications for work and issue dated receipts on their behalf.

4. Provision must also be made (wherever feasible) for workers to register applications for work through mobile telephones in addition to the MGNREGA website and this should feed in directly into the MIS. In case of mobile telephones, the system must be made convenient to illiterate workers and may include interactive voice response system (IVRS) and voice-enabled interactions. This option must automatically issue dated receipts.
5. State Governments will ensure that the MGNREGA MIS will record the demand for work. It will track (for each GP) the gap between date of application for work and date of opening of work.
6. MGNREGA software will automatically generate the pay order for payment of unemployment allowance to such wage seekers whose demand for work is not met within 15 days of demand. Reports prepared on this will have to be part of the essential set of reports to be tracked at the State level. (Source: Government of India, Ministry of Rural Development, Mihir Shah Committee (2012), *MGNREGA Operational Guidelines*.

10.12 Economic Survey, 2016-17 on MGNREGA

Reviewing the progress of MGNREGA, the *Economic Survey*, 2016-17 observed, 'The MGNREGS programme has evolved over the last two years to increase its focus on creation of durable assets, diversification of livelihood opportunities, selection of public works in congruence with other infrastructure programmes such as PMGSY and PMAY-Grameen and a greater thrust on natural resource management and agriculture and allied activities. This is expected to improve farmers' income and enlarge their wage opportunities. The programme is self-targeted. Often those who belong to deprived households and depend on casual labour are beneficiaries. The programme also provides a higher number of days of employment (150 days instead of 100 days) in drought affected areas.

Technological and programmatic improvements have been made in the last two years:

- MGNREGS job cards for 10.9 crore active workers was digitalized, of which 8.7 crore workers had their job cards seeded with Aadhaar.
- 4 crore workers were brought into the Aadhaar payment bridge.
- Nearly 39 lakh MGNREGS assets were geo-tagged since September 2016. These were provided publicly to improve accountability and transparency.
- 95 percent of MGNREGS wages were paid into beneficiary accounts, thereby, reducing scope for out-of-system leakage of wage payments.
- About 68 percent of active job cards were also verified and updated.

As a result, the number of completed works has increased from 25-30 lakhs (yearly average since inception) to 48 lakh in the current year. 70 percent of these works is in agriculture and allied activities (an increase from 50 percent in 2013-14). Additionally, participation of women in MGNREGS increased from 40 percent in 2006-2007 to 56 percent in 2016-17". [3]

10.13 MGNREGA in the 2017-18 Budget

Union Finance Minister Shri Arun Jaitley made the following observations in his Budget Speech to the Parliament on February 1, 2017, "Our Government has made a conscious effort to reorient MGNREGA to support our resolve to double farmers' income. While providing at least 100 days employment to every rural household, MGNREGA should create productive assets to improve farm productivity and incomes. The target of 5 lakh farm ponds and 10 lakh compost pits announced in the last Budget from MGNREGA funds will be fully achieved. In fact, against 5 lakh farm ponds, it is expected that about 10 lakh farm ponds would be completed by March 2017. During 2017-18, another 5 lakh farm ponds will be taken up. This single measure will contribute greatly to drought proofing of gram panchayats.

Participation of women in MGNREGA has increased to 55 percent from less than 48 percent in the past.

Honourable Members would be happy to note that the budget provision of ₹ 38,500 crores under MGNREGA in 2016-17 has been increased to ₹ 48,000 crores in 2017-18. This is the highest ever allocation for MGNREGA. The initiative to geo-tag all MGNREGA assets and putting them in public domain has established greater transparency. We are also using space technology in a big way to plan MGNREGA works". [4]

10.14 MGNREGA: Concluding Observations

Enactment of MGNREGA was a historic step in the Indian context. MGNREGA is visualized as a first step towards the realization of the economic right to work as envisioned in the Directive Principles of State Policy in the Constitution of India. It recognizes Article 39 of the Constitution, according to which the State must ensure that "citizens, men and women equally, have the right to an adequate means to livelihood" and Article 41 whereby "the State, shall within the limits of its economic capacity and development, make effective provision for securing Right to Work…"

The potential of the MGNREGA to lead the economy towards a labour-intensive growth path needs to be emphasized in this context. The wage-work programme needs to be seen in a long-term perspective, with a strong planning component, dovetailing it with the ongoing development efforts, incorporating decentralised planning and implementation, skill training, maintenance of public assets and eventually absorbing wage-earners into mainstream employment. The path towards full employment lies in strengthening the sectors where the poor are located and stabilizing their incomes, improving their asset base, constructing basic socio-economic infrastructure at the local level, enabling access to paid work opportunities and exerting an upward pressure on market wages. MGNREGA as a programme is expected to create conditions for realisation of the above outcomes.

According to some recent studies, the performance of MGNREGA varies significantly across the States. There are some States where MGNREGA has managed to achieve its key outcomes very well and which have indeed innovated in many respects. In others, performance has been unimpressive and lack lustre. Given that the overall framework for MGNREGA is similar across the States, the variations in performance depend on factors such as political and administrative will of the governments, historical background of the state as well as the nature of civil society and public actions around MGNREGA State Governments have the responsibility of framing the rules as well as overseeing the actual implementation of the scheme on the ground. There is a lot of scope for State Governments to innovate and adapt the scheme according to the local requirements. State-specific experiences are important sources for innovations which in turn provide valuable lessons for replication. The relative success of the scheme in some regions, and failure in others highlights the need to properly understand the reasons for inter- and intra-state variations and to replicate and adopt features of implementation of the better performing states.

In a number of states, low participation of women in the programme is not due to the lack of demand from women but to the social norms that restrict work participation outside the home, especially in states like Uttar Pradesh and Bihar. Thus, there are still several hurdles in most of the states for enhancing women's participation in the programme. One of the stated objectives of MGNREGA is to foster a sense of gender equality and encourage women's participation in the economic domain. However, such exclusion only leads to reinforcement of the existing social biases against women and goes against the spirit of MGNREGA. Fostering gender equality also implies that the state must step in to lighten the women's role in the *care economy*.

Overall, even within the existing framework and limitations, many of the problems can be substantially overcome if the political and administrative leadership at the state and local levels plays a more proactive role in implementing the objectives of the MGNREGA.

Endnotes

1. Government of India, Planning Commission, *An Approach to the Twelfth Five Year Plan*, October 2011, p. 5.
2. Ibid., pp. 60-61.
3. Government of India, Ministry of Finance, *Economic Survey*, 2016-17, p. 181.
4. Government of India, Ministry of Finance, Budget 2017-18, Speech of Shri Arun Jaitley, Minister of Finance, February 1, 2017, paras 34 to 36.

11

National Rural Livelihoods Mission (NRLM)—Aajeevika

Swarnjayanti Gram Swarozgar Yojana (SGSY) was restructured as National Rural Livelihoods Mission (NRLM) to implement it in a mission mode and in a phased manner for targeted and time-bound delivery of results. NRLM was renamed as Deendayal Antayodaya Yojana (DAY-NRLM) in November 2015.

NRLM aims to reduce poverty by enabling the poor households to access gainful self-employment and skilled wage employment opportunities, resulting in appreciable improvement in their livelihoods on a sustainable basis, through building strong grassroots institutions of the poor.

Universal social mobilization through formation of Self-help Groups (SHGs) under NRLM will ensure that at least one member of each rural BPL family, preferably a woman member, is covered under SHG net. With a view to form strong peoples institutions, NRLM focuses on setting up of federations of SHGs from village panchayat to district levels. NRLM proposes to ensure universal financial inclusion by facilitating opening of savings accounts of all its beneficiaries, simultaneously encouraging thrift and credit activities, facilitating access to credit from banks etc. There is a provision to utilize 10 percent of allocation under the programme for training and capacity building of the intended beneficiaries to take up the micro enterprises for enhancing their incomes. In addition to self-employment, NRLM also focuses on supporting rural BPL youth for accessing skilled wage employment through placement-linked skill development projects.

The two major strategic shifts under NRLM, vis-à-vis

SGSY, are: (a) NRLM is a demand-driven programme and the states will formulate their own poverty reduction action plans under it based on their past experience, resources and skills base and (b) NRLM provides for a professional support structure for programme implementation at all levels from national to sub-district level in different streams.

In order to ensure a holistic approach towards income enhancement of the rural poor, NRLM focuses on 4 streams of livelihoods which are as follows:

1. Coping with vulnerabilities: debt bondage, food insecurity, migration, health checks.
2. Existing livelihoods: stabilising and expanding, making them sustainable.
3. Self-employment: micro enterprise development, skilled wage employment.
4. Opportunities in growing sectors of the economy.

11.1 Main Provisions of NRLM

11.1.1 Universal Social Mobilization: To begin with, NRLM would ensure that at least one member from each identified rural poor household, preferably a woman, is brought under the self-help group (SHG) network in a time bound manner. Subsequently, both women and men would be organized for addressing livelihoods issues, i.e. farmers' organizations, milk producers' cooperatives, weavers' associations etc. All these institutions are inclusive and no poor would be left out of them. NRLM would ensure adequate coverage of vulnerable sections of the society such that 50 percent of the beneficiaries are SC/STs, 15 percent are minorities and 3 percent are persons with disability, while keeping in view the ultimate target of 100 percent coverage of BPL families.

11.1.2 Promotion of Institutions of the Poor: Strong institutions of the poor such as SHGs and their village level and higher level federations are necessary to provide space, voice and resources for the poor and for reducing their dependence on external agencies. They empower them and also act as instruments of knowledge and technology dissemination, and hubs of production, collectivization and commerce. NRLM, therefore, would focus on setting up these institutions at various levels.

In addition, NRLM would promote specialized institutions like livelihood collectives, producers' co-operatives and companies for livelihood promotion through deriving economies of scale, backward and forward linkages, and access to information, credit, technology, markets etc. The livelihoods collectives would enable the poor to optimize their limited resources.

There are existing institutions of the poor women formed by governments and NGOs. NRLM would strengthen all existing institutions of the poor in a partnership mode.

11.1.3 Training, Capacity Building and Skill Building: NRLM would ensure that the poor are provided with the requisite skills for managing their institutions, linking up with markets, managing their existing livelihoods, enhancing their credit absorption capacity and credit worthiness etc. A multi-pronged approach is envisaged for continuous capacity building of the targeted families, SHGs, their federations, government functionaries, bankers, NGOs and other key stakeholders. Particular focus would be on developing and engaging community professionals and community resource persons for capacity building of SHGs and their federations and other collectives. NRLM would make extensive use of information technology to make knowledge dissemination and capacity building more effective.

11.1.4 Revolving Fund and Capital Subsidy: Subsidy would be available in the form of revolving fund and capital subsidy. The revolving fund would be provided to the SHGs (where more than 70 percent members are from BPL households) as an incentive to inculcate the habit of thrift and accumulate their own funds towards meeting their credit needs in the long-run and immediate consumption needs in the short-run. Subsidy would be a corpus and used for meeting the credit needs of members directly and as catalytic capital for leveraging repeat bank finance. Capital subsidy fund would be given directly to the SHGs or would be routed to the SHGs through the federations, wherever the SHGs desire such an arrangement.

11.1.5 Universal Financial Inclusion: NRLM would work towards achieving universal financial inclusion, beyond basic banking services to all the poor households, SHGs and their federations. NRLM would work on both demand and supply side of financial inclusion. On the demand side, it would promote financial literacy among the poor and provide catalytic capital to the SHGs and their federations. On the supply side, it would coordinate with the financial sector and encourage use of information technology-based financial technologies, business correspondents and community facilitators. It would also work towards universal coverage of rural poor against loss of life, health and assets. Further, it would work on remittances, especially in areas where migration is endemic.

11.1.6 Provision of Interest Subsidy: The rural poor need credit at low rate of interest and in multiple doses to make their ventures economically viable. In order to ensure affordable credit, NRLM has a provision for subsidy on interest rate above 7 percent per annum for all eligible SHGs, who have availed loans from mainstream financial institutions, based on prompt loan repayment (This would not be applicable when a SHG avails capital subsidy. Interest subsidy would be provided to this SHG, when they avail a fresh loan after repaying the capital subsidy-linked loan). This subsidy would be available to SHGs, where at least 70 percent of the members are from BPL households, till a member accesses credit, through repeat cumulative loaning, up to ₹ 1 lakh per household.

11.1.7 Infrastructure Creation and Marketing Support: NRLM would seek to ensure that the infrastructure needs for the major livelihood activities of the poor are met with. It would also provide support for marketing to the institutions of the poor. The range of activities in marketing support includes market research, market intelligence, technology extension, developing backward and forward linkages, building livelihood collectives and supporting their business plans. NRLM would encourage and support partnerships with public and private organizations and their networks/associations for these activities, particularly for market linkages. 20 percent of the programme outlay of a state (25 percent in case of North-Eastern States and Sikkim) is reserved for this purpose.

11.1.8 Skills and Placement Projects: NRLM would scale up the existing skill and placement projects through partnership mode as one of the best investments in youth, and provide impetus to livelihood opportunities in emerging markets. For strengthening this, various models of partnerships with public, private, non-government and community organizations would be developed. A strong relationship would also be developed with industry associations and sector specific employers' associations. National Skill Development Corporation (NSDC) would be one of the leading partners in this effort. 15 percent of the central allocation under NRLM is earmarked for this purpose.

11.1.9 Rural Self-employment Training Institutes (RSETIs): NRLM encourages public sector banks to set up RSETIs in all districts of the country. RSETIs transform unemployed rural youth in the district into confident self-employed entrepreneurs through need-based experiential learning programme followed by systematic handholding support. Banks are completely involved in selection, training and post-training follow-up stages. RSETIs partner with others, including institutions of the poor, to realize their mandate and agenda.

11.1.10 Innovations: NRLM believes that successful innovations can reduce poverty. 5 percent of the Central allocation is, therefore, earmarked for innovations. Those innovations which have the potential for reaching out specifically to the poorest or for reaching out to the largest number of poor and having maximum impact with limited resources, would be preferred and supported.

11.1.11 Convergence: NRLM would place very high emphasis on convergence with other programmes of the Ministry of Rural Development and other Central Ministries and programmes of State Governments for developing synergies directly and through the institutions of the poor.

11.1.12 Partnerships with NGOs and other CSOs: NRLM would proactively seek partnerships with non-government organizations (NGOs) and other civil society organizations (CSOs), at two levels: strategic and implementation. The partnerships would be guided by core beliefs and values of NRLM, and mutual agreement on processes and outcomes. NRLM would develop a national framework for partnerships with NGOs and other CSOs. Further, NRLM would seek partnerships with various other stakeholders at various levels directly or through the institutions of the poor.

11.1.13 Linkages with PRIs: In view of the eminent roles of panchayat raj institutions (PRIs) that include governance, commercial and political, it is necessary to consciously structure and facilitate a mutually beneficial working relationship between panchayats and institutions of the poor, particularly at the level of village panchayats. Formal platforms would be established for regular consultations between such institutions and PRIs for exchange of mutual advice, support and sharing of resources. However, care would be taken to protect their autonomy. Where there are no PRIs, the linkages would be with traditional local village institutions.

11.1.14 Sensitive Support Structures: Process-intensive effort of NRLM would require dedicated human resources. Realizing this, NRLM would be setting up sensitive and dedicated support structures at the national, state, district and sub-district levels. NRLM Advisory, Coordination and Empowered Committees and National Mission Management Unit at the national level, State Rural Livelihood Missions (SRLMs) as autonomous bodies and State Mission Management Units at state level, District Mission Management

Units at district level, and sub-district units at block and/or cluster levels would constitute these support structures. The institutions of the poor, their staff and other social capital would also provide support. These support structures would be staffed with professionally competent and dedicated human resources through appropriate arrangements including partnerships and outsourcing of services.

11.1.15 Technical Support: NRLM would provide technical assistance to the states and all other partners for creating and strengthening their institutional capacities for its effective implementation. It would build national knowledge management and learning forums/systems. It would facilitate partnerships between institutions of the poor and banking sectors, public and private sectors, for ensuring last mile service delivery to reach the poor. It would build a national pool of experts, practitioners and advisers in all the relevant disciplines for providing handholding support to SRLMs for developing and executing state poverty reduction strategies.

11.2 Funding Pattern, Transition and Implementation

NRLM is a Centrally-sponsored scheme and financing of the programme would be shared between the Centre and the States in the ratio of 75:25 (90:10 in case of North-Eastern States including Sikkim; completely from the Centre in case of UTs). The Central allocation earmarked for the States would broadly be distributed in relation to the incidence of poverty in the States.

All States/UTs would have to transit to NRLM within a period of one year from the date of formal launch of NRLM.

NRLM would fund states against appraised and approved annual action plans and state perspective and implementation plans that outline the results and the processes towards these results. It would review the performance against these plans half-yearly and annually and funds flow to the states would be based on the revised annual plans.

11.3 Monitoring, Evaluation and Learning

NRLM is process-intensive and therefore, it would constantly review, assess and learn from the qualitative and quantitative progress achieved at various levels. A robust IT-based monitoring, evaluation and learning system would be in place to facilitate learning and continuous improvement and support informed decision making at all levels.

NRLM would put in place various mechanisms for monitoring:

1. Accountability in institutions of the poor includes institutional self-monitoring, peer internal audit of processes and local social audit.
2. Management information system (MIS) based input-output monitoring includes results framework-based MIS; milestones linked to investments/inputs; web-based MIS; real time input-output monitoring at various levels; and MIS with data of partners.
3. IT-framework for dedicated digital grid includes national database of poor, their institutions, and skill development (jobs/self-employment), national livelihood portal, communication/knowledge dissemination channels, thematic e-groups etc.
4. Internal review mechanisms at various levels.
5. External social audit, public expenditure tracking and community score cards.
6. Impact Assessment—state level baseline assessments and external interim impact evaluation studies of progress on key result indicators; independent national assessment of household level well-being through panel studies at periodic intervals and periodic thematic national assessments.
7. SRLM Annual Reports and NRLM Annual Report.
8. NRLM would put in place a comprehensive financial management system at SRLM to ensure transparency, efficiency and accountability. NRLM would position an IT-based fund tracking system and promote e-book

keeping in institutions of the poor and in support structures.

11.4 Mahlla Kissan Shasaktikaran Pariyojana (MKSP)

In order to improve the present status of women in agriculture, and to enhance the opportunities for their empowerment, Government of India has announced MKSP as a sub-component of NRLM. MKSP recognizes the centrality of women in agriculture and therefore aims to provide direct and indirect support to enable them to achieve sustainable agriculture production. It will initiate a learning cycle by which women are enabled to learn and adopt appropriate technologies and farming systems. MKSP will be implemented as a sub-component of NRLM through specially formulated projects.

The salient features of MKSP are as follows:

1. Primary objective of MKSP is to empower women in agriculture by making systematic investments to enhance their participation and productivity in agriculture-based livelihood.
2. Through this scheme, it is proposed to create sustainable agricultural livelihood opportunities for women in agriculture and in the process ensure food and nutrition security at the household and the community levels.
3. Under MKSP, community-based women institutions in the rural area will be strengthened in order to enable them to manage their agriculture-based livelihood activities.
4. Under MKSP, use of locally-adopted resource conserving, farmer-led and environmentally-friendly technologies has been emphasized.
5. Ministry of Rural Development, Government of India would provide funding support or up to 75 percent (90 percent for North-East and hill states) to the project submitted by the State Government/project implementing agencies (PIAs) under MKSP. Balance is to be contributed by the respective State Governments or any other donor

agencies.

The expected outcomes of MKSP are as follows:

1. Net increase in the income of women in agriculture on a sustainable basis.
2. Improvement in food and nutritional security of women in agriculture and their families.
3. Increase in area under cultivation, cropping intensity and food production by women.
4. Increased levels of skill and performance by women in agriculture.
5. Increased access of women in agriculture to productive land, inputs, credit, technology and information.
6. Drudgery reduction for women in agriculture through use or gender friendly tools/technologies.
7. Increased access to market and market information for better marketing of their product.
8. Increased soil health and fertility to sustain agriculture based livelihoods.
9. Increased visibility of women in agriculture as an interest group.

11.5 Twelfth Five Year Plan (2012-17) on NRLM

Pointing out the focus of NRLM, the Approach to the Twelfth Plan observed, "The experience with MGNREGA has clearly highlighted the problems that are often encountered when a programme is universalised without sufficient preparatory work and support systems being in place. This has been a problem with the SGSY scheme also. While the fast growth of the SHG-Bank Linkage (SBL) model is heartening, there are also many concerns. A large part of the problem derives from the top-down, target-driven approach that has undermined the demand-driven thrust, which was the original mandate. There are also reports of high rates of mortality in many SHGs, which has had an adverse impact on the credibility of the SBL model in the eyes of key stakeholders, including potential women members, as also bankers.

The real power of the SBL model lies in the economies of scale created by Self Help Group (SHG) Federations (comprising 150-200 SHGs each). This is evident, for example, in bulk purchase of inputs (seeds, fertilisers etc.) and marketing of outputs (crops, vegetables, milk, NTFPs etc.). They can also provide larger loans for housing and health facilities to their members by tying up with large service or loan providers. A variety of insurance services can also be made available, including life, health, livestock and weather insurance. It has also been shown how doing business with SHG Federations can help public sector bank branches in remote rural areas become viable entities.

Taking a cue from the lessons of the SGSY experience, the Government of India has launched the National Rural Livelihoods Mission in 2011. There is a clear understanding that the SBL programme can only be successful if it is tied up with livelihood programmes such as improved agriculture, dairying, marketing, etc. Thus, the SBL and livelihood programmes are complementary to each other and their simultaneous implementation is the key to poverty alleviation. Incomes earned through livelihood initiatives need to be saved. Of these savings, women are the best custodians. These savings must, in turn, be reinvested in livelihood options that raise incomes, setting up a virtuous cycle. The distinctive focus of the NRLM is on Federations of SHGs that become powerful units of economic empowerment, enabling the poor to radically alter the balance of power in the markets they participate in as both producers and consumers". [1]

In short, NRLM aims at organizing all rural poor households and continuously nurturing and supporting them till they emerge out of abject poverty, by organizing one woman member from each household into affinity-based women self-help groups (SHGs) and their federations at village and higher levels by 2024-25. The objective is to ensure that each family, once it is in the SHG network for a period of 6-8 years is able to achieve household food security and have 3-4 stabilized livelihoods through a strong convergence with panchayati raj institutions (PRIs).

Endnote

1. Government of India, Planning Commission, *An Approach to the Twelfth Five Year Plan*, October 2011, pp. 61-62.

12

National Urban Livelihoods Mission (NULM)

Ministry of Housing and Urban Poverty Alleviation, Government of India had been implementing a Centrally-sponsored scheme called Swarna Jayanti Shahari Rozgar Yojana (SJSRY) since 1997 which was restructured as Deendayal Antayodaya Yojana—National Urban Livelihoods Mission (DAY-NULM) in September, 2013. SJSRY aimed to provide gainful employment to the urban unemployed and underemployed.

The NULM has been under implementation w.e.f. September 24, 2013 in all district headquarters (irrespective of population) and all the cities with population of 1 lakh or more. It focuses on organizing urban poor in SHGs, creating opportunities for skill development leading to market-based employment, and helping them set up self-employment ventures by ensuring easy access to credit. The mission aims at providing shelter with basic amenities to urban homeless. It also plans to address livelihood concerns of urban street vendors.

12.1 Urbanization and Livelihood

Economic development and urbanisation are closely linked. Cities in India are emerging as the country's engines of economic growth.

The urban informal sector comprises a large part of the unorganized non-agriculture sector. Low levels of education and skill in the unorganized sector workers have resulted in their inability to access the opportunities offered by emerging markets. This underscores the criticality of skills up-gradation for better livelihoods opportunities in urban areas.

Most of the poor are involved in informal sector activities where there is a constant threat of eviction, removal, confiscation of goods and almost non-existent social security cover. Even when segments of the urban population are not income-poor, they face deprivation in terms of lack of access to sanitary living conditions and their well-being is hampered by discrimination, social exclusion, crime, violence, insecurity of tenure, hazardous environmental conditions and lack of voice in governance.

The dimensions of urban poverty can be broadly divided into three categories:

- Residential vulnerability (access to land, shelter, basic services, etc.).
- Social vulnerability (deprivations related to factors like gender, age and social stratification, lack of social protection, inadequate voice and participation in governance structures etc.).
- Occupational vulnerability (precarious livelihoods, dependence on informal sector for employment and earnings, lack of job security, poor working conditions, etc.).

These vulnerabilities are inter-related. Amongst the urban poor, there are sections subject to greater vulnerability in terms of the above classification. These include women, children, and the aged, SCs, STs, minorities and differently-abled persons who deserve attention on a priority basis.

The National Urban Housing and Habitat Policy (NUHHP), 2007 aims to promote sustainable development of habitat in the country with a view to ensure equitable supply of land, shelter and services at affordable prices to all sections of the society. The most vulnerable of these are the urban homeless who live with no shelter or social security/protection. Recent pronouncements of the Supreme Court of India have brought into focus the plight of the urban homeless by holding that the right to dignified shelters is a necessary component of the right to life under Article 21 of the Constitution of India. There is, therefore, a need to develop a policy and programme for the urban homeless.

Urban poverty being multi-dimensional, various

vulnerabilities faced by the poor in cities and towns—occupational, residential and social—need to be addressed simultaneously in a comprehensive and integrated manner with a targeted focus on the vulnerable groups so that a definitive impact can be made on ground. Residential vulnerability issues are being addressed through Prime Minister Awaas Yojana (Urban). The other two vulnerabilities, viz. occupational and social can be best addressed by creating opportunities for skill development leading to market-based employment and helping them to set up self-employment ventures. Urban poverty alleviation programmes need to be based on skill development and easy access to credit.

It is in this context that a mission-mode approach to urban livelihoods was considered necessary in the form of the National Urban Livelihoods Mission (NULM).

12.2 NULM Mission Statement

NULM aims to reduce poverty and vulnerability of the urban poor households by enabling them to access gainful self-employment and skilled wage employment opportunities, resulting in an appreciable improvement in their livelihoods on a sustainable basis, through building strong grassroots level institutions of the poor. NULM would aim at providing shelter equipped with essential services to the urban homeless in a phased manner. In addition, it would also address livelihood concerns of the urban street vendors by facilitating access to suitable spaces, institutional credit, social security and skills to the urban street vendors for accessing emerging market opportunities.

12.3 Guiding Principles and Values of NULM

The core belief of NULM is that the poor are entrepreneurial and have innate desire to come out of poverty. The challenge is to unleash their capabilities to generate meaningful and sustainable livelihoods. The first step in this process is motivating the urban poor to form their own institutions. They and their institutions need to be provided sufficient capacity so that they can manage the external environment, access finance, expand their skills, enterprises and assets. This requires continuous and carefully designed handholding support. An external, dedicated and sensitive support structure, from the national level to the city and community levels, is required to induce social mobilisation, institution building and livelihood promotion.

NULM believes that any livelihood promotion programme can be scaled up in a time-bound manner only if driven by the poor and their institutions. Such strong institutional platforms support the poor in building up their own human, social, financial, and other assets. This, in turn, enables them access to rights, entitlements, opportunities and services from the public and private sectors, while enhancing their solidarity, voice and bargaining power.

As per the Constitution (74th Amendment) Act, 1992, urban poverty alleviation is a legitimate function of the Urban Local Bodies (ULB). Therefore, ULBs would need to undertake a lead role for all issues and programmes concerning the urban poor in cities/towns, including skills and livelihoods.

NULM aims at universal coverage of the urban poor for skill development and credit facilities. It strives for skills training of the urban poor for market-based jobs and self-employment, facilitating easy access to credit.

Street vendors constitute an important segment of the urban population at the bottom of the pyramid. Street vending provides a source of self-employment, and thus acts as a measure of urban poverty alleviation without major Government intervention. They have a prominent place in the urban supply chain and are an integral part of the economic growth process within urban areas. NULM aims at facilitating access to suitable spaces, institutional credit, social security and skills to the urban street vendors for accessing emerging market opportunities.

Urban homeless persons who live without shelter or social security/protection are the most vulnerable class, even while they contribute towards sustaining cities with their cheap labour. Life on the streets involves surviving continuously at the edge, in a physically brutalized and challenging environment. There is a need for appropriate policy intervention to address the challenges faced by homeless people, with regard to shelter, social housing and social protection. Accordingly, NULM aims at providing shelter equipped with essential services to the urban homeless in a phased manner.

NULM places a very high emphasis on convergence with schemes/programmes of the relevant line Ministries and programmes of state governments dealing with skills, livelihoods, entrepreneurship development, health, education, social assistance etc. An alliance strategy is sought with all concerned departments to promote skills training of rural-urban migrants as a bridge between the livelihoods of the rural and urban poor.

NULM aims at partnership with the private sector in providing skill training, employment and operation of shelter for homeless. It strives for active participation of private and civil society sectors in providing shelter to the urban homeless, skill training and placement of the urban poor and also in facilitating technological, marketing and handholding support for the urban poor entrepreneurs who want to be self-employed and set up their own small businesses or manufacturing units.

NULM espouses the following values:

1. Ownership and productive involvement of the urban poor and their institutions in all processes.
2. Transparency in programme design and implementation, including institution-building and capacity strengthening.
3. Accountability of government functionaries and the community.
4. Partnerships with industry and other stakeholders.
5. Community self-reliance, self-dependence, self-help and mutual-help.

12.4 Strategies of NULM

NULM has adopted the following strategies:

1. Building capacity of the urban poor, their institutions and the machinery involved in the implementation of livelihoods development and poverty alleviation programmes through handholding support.
2. Enhancing and expanding existing livelihoods options of the urban poor.
3. Building skills to enable access to growing market-based job opportunities offered by emerging urban economies.
4. Training for and support to the establishment of micro enterprises by the urban poor.
5. Ensuring availability and access for the urban homeless population to permanent 24-hour shelters including the basic infrastructural facilities like water supply, sanitation, safety and security.
6. Catering to the needs of especially vulnerable segments of the urban homeless like the dependent children, aged, disabled, mentally ill, and recovering patients etc., by creating special sections within homeless shelters and provisioning special service linkages for them.
7. Establishing strong rights-based linkages with other programmes which cover the right of the urban homeless to food, healthcare, education etc. and ensure access for homeless populations to various entitlements, including social security pensions, sanitation, identity, financial inclusion, school admission etc. and affordable housing.
8. Addressing livelihood concerns of the urban street vendors by facilitating access to suitable spaces, institutional credit, social security and skills to the urban street vendors for accessing emerging market opportunities.

The primary target of NULM is the urban poor, including the urban homeless.

12.5 Social Mobilisation and Institution Development

The mobilisation of urban poor households to form their

own institutions is an important investment for an effective and sustainable poverty reduction programme. NULM envisages universal social mobilisation of urban poor into self-help groups (SHGs) and their federations. At least one member from each urban poor household, preferably a woman, should be brought under the SHGs network in a time-bound manner. These groups will serve as a support system for the poor, to meet their financial and social needs. Normally, women SHGs will be formed, but male SHGs of handicapped persons will also be allowed to be formed.

NULM would lay particular emphasis on the mobilisation of vulnerable sections of the urban population such as SCs, STs, minorities, female-headed households, persons with disabilities, the destitute, migrant labourers, and especially vulnerable occupational groups such as street vendors, rag pickers, domestic workers, beggars, construction workers etc.

12.5.1 Building Community Institutions (SHGs and Their Federations): For catalysing the formation of SHGs and their federations and to promote the financial inclusion of SHG members under NULM, resource organisations (ROs) will be engaged to facilitate the formation of SHGs, their development and bank-linkages, formation of their federations at the area and city levels, training and capacity building, and establishing links to ULBs and to mitigate social, occupational and residential vulnerabilities.

Autonomous registered agencies set up by State or Central Government or well established long-standing federations of SHGs having significant experience in managing large-scale community driven programmes and developing successful implementation strategies in social moblisation and institution building in urban or rural areas may be preferred as ROs.

In addition, non-government organisations (NGOs) may be selected as a ROs on the basis of strict criteria including registration status of the NGO, turnover, number of years of experience, sound procurement and financial management capacity, number of dedicated expert staff, domain knowledge and prior experience in social moblisation of poor households, training and capacity building, livelihood promotion, and bank linkage of the community organisations.

A maximum of ₹ 10,000 can be spent per self-help group for its formation, handholding up to two years, training of all the members, bank linkage, formation of federation and other related activities. States will be expected to enter into an agreement with ROs and payment will be made on the basis of milestones like SHG formation, training of members, bank linkage, formation of federation at the area and city levels and access to benefits under NULM, including revolving fund. ROs will handhold the SHG for a period up to two years.

Services of ASHA/Anganwadi workers and other community level functionaries under various schemes of the Central and State Governments may also be utilised at the field level to facilitate the formation of SHGs under NULM.

12.5.2 Universal Financial Inclusion: NULM aims to achieve universal financial inclusion, through opening of basic savings accounts, facilitating access to financial literacy, credit, affordable insurance, and remittance facilities to the urban poor and their institutions. It will also co-ordinate with financial institutions to encourage the use of ICT-based technologies, financial correspondents and community facilitators like *Bank Mitras* and *Bima Mitras* for the benefit of the urban poor. In particular, NULM will facilitate coverage of urban poor households under schemes such as Rashtriya Swasthya Bima Yojana (RSBY), Jan Shree Bima Yojana (JSBY) and similar programmes.

12.5.3 Revolving Fund Support to SHGs and Their Federations: NULM envisages that Thrift and Credit (T&C), functional literacy and basic skills training would be the main trinity of activities of Self-help Groups (SHGs). A revolving fund support to the tune of ₹ 10,000 per SHG will be provided to SHGs with more than 70 percent urban poor members and those, which have not availed such support earlier. This revolving fund is to be given only to those SHGs who have been doing thrift and credit activities for at least six months.

A revolving fund support of ₹ 50,000 would be available to a registered area level federation (ALF) to sustain their activities.

12.5.4 City Livelihood Centres (CLCs): The objective of CLCs is to provide a platform whereby the urban poor can market their services and access information and other benefits. CLCs will act as a *one-stop shop* for those seeking services from the informal sector as well as for the urban poor promoting their services and products.

CLCs will be positioned as a resource centre for those seeking information relating to employment and skills training opportunities etc. The centres may give the poor access to information on market demand, skills training programmes offered and placement opportunities. For those seeking skills training, wage employment or aiming to establish and sustain self-employment ventures, CLCs can facilitate necessary guidance, counselling and technical support.

12.5.5 Training and Other Capacity Building Schemes for SHGs and Their Federations: This component will be used for training and capacity building of SHGs and their federations on various issues like bank linkage, book keeping and accounts, micro-planning, micro-investment process, roles and responsibilities of members etc. The component will be implemented by national, state and city resources centres/agencies including civil society organisations, and Mission Management Units at various levels.

12.6 Capacity Building and Training (CB&T)

A key objective of CB&T is to transform the role of the Ministry of Housing and Urban Poverty Alleaviation and State Agencies in charge of urban poverty alleviation into providers of high quality technical assistance in the fields of urban livelihoods promotion and urban poverty alleviation.

12.6.1 Technical Support at National, State and City Levels: The objective of this is to establish timely and high quality technical assistance at Central, State and City levels to roll out and implement NULM.

A National Mission Management Unit (NMMU) will be established at the Centre. Additionally, support to states and cities would be provided for setting-up of State Mission Management Unit (SMMU) and City Mission Management Unit (CMMU) with good quality livelihood and programme management professionals and developing efficient institutional systems like HR, MIS, financial management, procurement, and social management. Technical support would also be provided to the states/cities to undertake comprehensive situational analysis to capture various dimensions of urban poverty in the state/cities. This would help states to prioritize interventions and resources while formulating state/city urban poverty reduction strategy/action plans. Specific technical assistance in each of programmatic themes would be offered to provide implementation support to states/cities/towns for achieving NULM outcomes.

12.6.2 Training and Other Capacity Building Schemes for Mission Management Units (MMUs): This will be used for training and capacity building of the technical resource persons of the MMUs at national, state and city levels. It will be implemented by national, state and city resources centres/agencies including civil society organisations, and MMUs at various levels.

12.7 Employment through Skills Training and Placement (EST&P)

This component of NULM will focus on providing assistance for development/upgrading of the skills of the urban poor so as to enhance their capacity for self-employment and salaried employment. EST&P intends to provide training to the urban poor as per the skill demand from the market, so that they can set up self-employment ventures or secure salaried employment. EST&P will target the urban poor subjected to occupational vulnerability. No minimum or maximum educational qualification is prescribed for the selection of beneficiaries under EST&P. The percentage of women beneficiaries under EST&P shall not be less than 30 percent. SCs and STs must be benefited at least to the extent of the proportion of their strength in the city/town population of poor. A special provision of 3 percent reservation should be made for the differently-abled under this programme. In view of the Prime Minister's 15-Point Programme for the Welfare of Minorities, at least 15 percent of the physical and financial targets under this component shall be earmarked for the minority communities. Apart from that, special attention will be paid to the skill upgradation of vulnerable groups like beggars, rag pickers, construction workers, destitute etc.

Skill training will be linked to accreditation and certification and preferably be undertaken on a public-private-partnership (PPP) basis. It will involve reputed institutes, including industrial training institutes (ITIs), polytechnics, industry associations, engineering colleges, management institutes, skill training centres, foundations, and other reputed entities in government, private and civil society sectors. The selection of these institutes/agencies to impart skills training shall be subject to a transparent process/verification of brand image and the quality of instructions being imparted.

Given the diversity of local contexts, each State will decide the skills important for their local economies. Apart from hard skills, training on soft skills should also be provided as a part of the same training programme. This may include spoken English, financial literacy, computer literacy, life skills including training on office and social etiquette, punctuality etc.

12.8 Self-employment Programme (SEP)

This component will focus on financial assistance to individuals/groups of urban poor for setting up gainful self-employment ventures/micro-enterprises, suited to their skills, training, aptitude and local conditions. The under-employed and unemployed urban poor will be encouraged to set up small enterprises relating to manufacturing, servicing and petty business for which there is considerable local demand. Local skills and local crafts should be particularly encouraged. Each city/town should develop a compendium of such activities keeping in view skills available, marketability of products, costs, economic viability etc. No minimum or maximum educational qualification is prescribed for the selection of beneficiaries under SEP. The percentage of women beneficiaries under SEP shall not be less than 30 percent. SCs and STs must be benefited at least to the extent of the proportion of their strength in the city/town population of poor. A special provision of 3 percent reservation should be made for the differently-abled under this programme. In view of the Prime Minister's 15-Point Programme for the Welfare of Minorities, at least 15 percent of the physical and financial targets under this component shall be earmarked for the minority communities.

Under this component, setting up of both individual and group micro enterprises will be supported. The project cost ceiling will be ₹ 2 lakh for individual enterprises and ₹ 10 lakh for group enterprises. Individual and groups may be provided loan from the banks and the application for such loans be preferably recommended by the SHGs.

Interest subsidy over and above 7 percent rate of interest will be available on a bank loan for setting up of an individual or group enterprise. No collateral is envisaged other than the micro enterprise itself.

Technology, marketing, consultancy and other support may also be provided by states/cities to beneficiaries in setting up micro enterprises, in relation to input procurement, production, packaging, branding, marketing etc. This may include provision of selling places for poor street vendors in the form of kiosks and rehri markets, weekend markets/festival bazaars/evening markets etc. in municipal grounds or on road sides on one hand and technical assistance with regard to market potential survey, input procurement, joint brand naming/designing, advertising, marketing etc. on the other.

12.9 Support to Urban Street Vendors

This component aims at skilling of street vendors, support micro-enterprise development, credit enablement and pro-vending urban planning along with supporting social security options for vulnerable groups such as women, SCs/STs and minorities. Up to 5 percent of the total NULM budget will be spent on this component.

Under NULM, states and cities will conduct a periodic socio-economic survey of street vendors, register street vendors and will issue Identity cards for street vendors. A database of street vendors will be development and maintained at each city. This will enable States/ULBs to prepare pro-vending urban planning and provide space for street vending.

Poor street vendors in urban areas can access skill training under the EST&P component of NULM and micro-enterprise development support under the SEP component of NULM.

Street vendors will be encouraged to access basic banking services. Additionally, efforts will be made to cover individual beneficiaries with credit cards so as to enable street vendors access for working capital and other purposes.

Street vendors will be encouraged to access other social security benefits available to them through various schemes of the Government of India, state-level and city-level social security and social assistance initiatives/schemes.

12.10 Scheme of Shelter for Urban Homeless (SUH)

The main objective of SUH is to provide shelter and all other essential services to the poorest of the poor segment of urban societies. The shelters should be permanent all-weather 24x7 shelters for the urban homeless. For every 1 lakh urban population, provisions should be made for permanent community shelters for a minimum of one hundred persons. Depending upon local conditions each shelter could cater to between 50 and 100 persons.

Priority would be given to cities with population above 1 million in census of 2011, and other cities and towns identified by the Government of India/State Governments to be of special social, historical or tourist importance.

Shelters should be a space for convergence and provisions of various entitlements of social security, food, education and health care systems. All homeless persons, in shelters should be given priority under various schemes, and Government programmes. This is because the homeless are unable to access many services due to lack of documentary proof such as address and birth proof etc.

Location should be close to homeless concentrations and work sites as far as practicable. They may be located close to the areas where the poorest congregate like railway stations, bus depots, terminals, markets, wholesale mandis etc.

Where existing infrastructure/public buildings are being used, suitable refurbishment and augmentation to meet requisite services/space requirement should be done. Permanent shelters may be built of concrete or durable and weather proof alternate structures. The State Governments will be encouraged to adopt innovative designs for low cost and energy efficient buildings.

13

Prime Minister Employment Generation Programme (PMEGP)

PMEGP was announced by the Prime Minister of India on August 15, 2008 in his address from Red Fort. It was launched by merging the Rural Employment Generation Programme (REGP) and Prime Minister's Rozgar Yojana (PMRY). It aims at creating employment opportunities in both urban and rural areas. KVIC is the Nodal Agency at National Level.

13.1 Objectives

PMEGP has the following objectives:

1. To generate continuous and sustainable employment opportunities in Rural and Urban areas of the country.
2. To provide continuous and sustainable employment to a large segment of traditional and prospective artisans, rural and urban unemployed youth in the country through setting up of micro enterprises.
3. To facilitate participation of financial institutions for higher credit flow to micro sector.

13.2 Eligibility

Following are eligible for the PMEGP:

1. Individuals above 18 years of age.
2. VIII Standard pass required for project above ₹ 10 lakh in manufacturing and above ₹ 5 lakh for service sector.
3. Self-help groups and charitable trusts.
4. Institutions registered under Societies Registration Act, 1860.
5. Production-based co-operative societies.

13.3 Salient Features

These are as under:

1. The scheme is implemented through KVIC and State/UT Khadi and Village Industries Boards in rural areas and through District Industries Centres in Urban and rural areas in the ratio of 30:30:40 between KVIC/KVIB/DIC respectively.
2. No income ceiling for setting up of projects.
3. Assistance under the scheme is available only to new units to be established.
4. Existing units or units already availed any government subsidy either under State/Central Government schemes are not eligible.
5. Any industry including coir-based projects excluding those mentioned in the negative list.
6. Per capita investment should not exceed ₹ 1 lakh in plain areas and ₹ 1.5 lakh in hilly areas.
7. Maximum project cost of ₹ 25 lakh in manufacturing sector and ₹ 10 lakh in service sector.

13.4 Area of Operation

Rural areas as declared under KVIC Act, 2006 and Scheme to be implemented by KVIC, KVIB and DIC.

(Rural area means the area comprised in any village and includes the area comprised in any town, the population of which does not exceed twenty thousand or such other figure as the Central Government may specify from time to time as declared under KVIC Act, 2006).

Urban Area: Only district industries centres (DICs).

13.5 Negative List of Activities

1. Industry/business connected with productions, processing, sale of meat or intoxicant items like beedi, pan, cigar, cigarette etc.
2. Industry/business connected with cultivation, sericulture, horticulture, floriculture.
3. Manufacture of polythene carry bags of less than 20 microns/containers of recycled plastic.
4. Processing of pashmina wool and products involving hand

spinning and hand weaving coming under purview of khadi certification rule.

5. Rural transport (except auto rickshaw, house boat, tourist boat in A&N Islands and except house boat, Shikara and tourist boats in Jammu and Kashmir and cycle rickshaw).
6. CNG auto rickshaw will be allowed only in A&N Islands and NER with the approval of chief secretary of the State on merit.

13.6 Quantum of Subsidy

It is as shown in Table 13.1.

Table 13.1: Quantum of Margin Money Subsidy

Categories of beneficiaries under PMEGP	Beneficiary's own contribution of project cost (percent)	Rate of subsidy (percent)	
		Urban	Rural
General category	10	15	25
Special (including SCs, STs, OBCs, minorities, women, ex-servicemen, physically handicapped, NER, hill and border areas.	5	25	35

13.7 E-tracking under PMEGP

1. To bring in transparency in implementation of PMEGP scheme as well as to create data base of PMEGP beneficiaries, e-tracking of PMEGP applications introduced.
2. Focus on first in first served (FIFS) in the processing of applications at all stages.
3. The system ensures complete transparency in the decision processes, leads to better governance and prevents corruption in implementation.

14

National Career Service (NCS) Project

India's economy has grown impressively in recent years. The country is poised to grow even faster, with its demographic potential, high investment and savings rates, and allocation of resources for infrastructure. But its high pace of economic growth and notable progress in reducing poverty over the last decade contrasts with the persistent gaps in creating a more inclusive, productive and formal labour market. Investment in skills development will ensure that economic and employment growth is more inclusive. This is especially important in the context of India's demographic transition that has also produced a youth bulge in the working age population.

India has a significant advantage of a young population and a declining dependency ratio, offering huge potential for a demographic dividend. There are, however, challenges which need to be addressed for fully reaping this unique dividend in the global scenario. Although the annual rate of growth of the Indian economy is one of the highest in the world, the growth in jobs is much less than the growth of the economy.

National Career Service (NCS) project is an initiative of the Ministry of Labour and Employment, Government of India for establishing quick and efficient career-related services.

Prime Minister Shri Narendra Modi launched the National Career Service programme on July 20, 2015 at the Forty-sixth Labour Conference with an objective of supporting varied stakeholders with better career information, easily available jobs and other employment-related services. Its vision is to provide a national platform for interface between stakeholders for responsive, transparent and efficient employment services in order to meet skill needs of a dynamic economy. The NCS programme is accessible through web and provides a large number of employment-related services to the Indian citizens. These services are supported by a toll free no 1800-425-1514 and are accessible through a network of common service centres and model career centres etc. It provides various career-related services like job search, career counselling, information on skill training programs/career options, job postings, organizing and participating in job fairs, finding blue collared local service providers (LSPs) like plumbers, electricians etc.

The key success factors of NCS initiative revolve around strengthening the existing employment exchange ecosystem with an ICT-enabled platform and reaching out to masses through multiple delivery channels and partnerships with existing job market players. Caught in a vicious cycle of decreasing job seeker registrations and vacancy notifications by employers, employment exchanges needed a transformation for better delivery of employment services. Employment exchanges have been transformed to focus more on counselling-related needs of candidates with establishment of career centres.

NCS is the converging point for Government of India's three major initiatives, namely Skill India, Digital India and Make in India, that aim to provide skilled manpower, improve digital infrastructure and generate employment opportunities for all.

14.1 Key Aspects of the NCS Project

With this background, NCS has been conceptualized as a comprehensive, multi-pronged, transformational project. Key aspects of this project include the following:

1. Establishment of career centres which would be enabled by making the right infrastructure and linkages available to perform counselling functions.
2. Implementation of a comprehensive capacity building initiative for augmenting the skills of career centre professionals and other ecosystem counselling partners.
3. Setting up a National Portal which will act as a platform to

bridge the gap between Government and private job providing ecosystem, job seeker and skill development ecosystem.

4. Providing access to tools to analyse skill-wise demand of industry and supply of jobseekers, as well as access to a rich knowledge repository of career counselling content in multiple languages so that candidates are counselled appropriately.
5. Collaboration with various stakeholders like State Governments, schools, colleges, jobseekers, skill development institutions, employers, NGOs, volunteer agencies, technology partners, verification agencies etc.
6. Establishing institutional/governance structures and Revenue Model for securing sustainability and relevance of the services being offered through these centres.
7. Appropriate information, education and communication (IEC) strategies to reach out to the stakeholders.

14.2 Focus Areas

NCS initiative aims to address the gaps in the employment market by strategic interventions for improving decent employment, enhancing quality of workforce, enhancing female labour force participation, entrepreneurial endeavours, informal to formal transition, engaging with rural workforce for higher productivity, and re-employment (second life) opportunities etc.

The focus areas for the NCS platform are listed below:

1. Enhancing career and employment opportunities.
2. Counselling and guidance for career development.
3. Focusing on decent employment.
4. Enhancing quality of workforce.
5. Enhancing female labour force participation.
6. Encouraging entrepreneurial endeavours.
7. Focusing on inclusive growth initiatives.
8. Engaging with rural workforce for higher productivity.
9. Re-employment opportunities for retired workforce.

10. Transition of workforce from informal to formal sectors.

The above list is indicative (and not exhaustive) and the Central Government may add to this list from time-to-time based on the needs of the economy and society for improving the employment market. Specific interventions could be designed on the NCS for one or more of the above focus areas.

14.3 Services Offered

Under the NCS initiative, the NCS Portal (www.ncs.gov.in) will be the platform where the various stakeholders will be interacting for exchange of career and employment-related opportunities. The counsellors empanelling with the Directorate General of Employment (DGE), Ministry of Labour and Employment, will offer the various services through this platform and leverage the network of career centres (employment exchanges) in the delivery of these services some of which are listed below:

1. **Online Registration of Candidates:**

- PAN/Aadhaar-based verification.
- Search for vacancies, counsellors etc.
- Rich repository of career content.
- Participation in job fairs.
- Seeking counselling and guidance services.

2. **Online Registration of Establishments:**

- Posting and managing job vacancies.
- Search for skilled workforce.
- Participation in job fairs.

3. **Online Registration of Counsellors and Guidance Experts:**

- PAN/Aadhaar-based verification.
- Providing counselling/guidance services.

4. **Online Registration of Local Service Providers (Plumbers, Drivers, Electricians etc.).**
5. **Multiple Delivery Channels:**

- Employment exchanges (career centres).
- Common service centres (CSCs).

- Internet and mobile-based access.

6. **Value Added Services Like Updates, Notifications, Alerts through SMS, E-mail, and IVRS etc.**
7. **Multi-lingual Call Centre (1800-425-1514) Services for Helping Candidates and Establishments in Registration, Profile Updation etc.**

14.4 Career Counselling

The Government is now giving increased focus on career counselling as a key activity of NCS to enable aspiring youth to pursue the right career choice according to their aptitude so that they join the workforce with better skills for enhancing growth and development. It has a vision to develop career centres as a real exchange platform for job seekers and providers. There is also a need to evolve a road map to make these centres tie-up with educational institutions and potential industries.

NCS aims to create a network of career counsellors on the NCS platform where the career centres will be the hub of counselling services. The services will include administration of psychometric tests to assess the student's/job seeker's personality/aptitude/interest etc. These tests would be made available via both online and offline modes. The NCS Portal provides an opportunity to browse through the list of the approved counsellors and book an appointment with them. Counselling services would be made available on face-to-face basis or via online platforms depending upon the chosen medium. The main aim of career counselling is to assist the job seekers in choosing a field that is in tune with their skills and their career expectations. The NCS Project also envisages offering vocational guidance services through empanelled vocational guidance (VG) experts, having requisite experience and expertise.

An integral component of the NCS Project is the establishment of model career centres (MCCs) in collaboration with the States. MCCs will have adequate facilities and infrastructure for delivery of various services to the stakeholders and can be subsequently replicated at other locations.

The NCS makes available a rich repository of career content on over 3,000 occupations across 52 sectors. The services under NCS are available online and can be accessed directly, through career centres, common service centres, mobile devices, cyber cafes etc. A dedicated helpdesk (multi-lingual) is also available from Tuesday to Sunday on 1800-425-1514 for assisting users.

14.5 Career Centres

NCS Project is focussed on establishing career centres in a phased approach ensuring that standardized set of services are offered all across.

14.5.1 Objectives: Career centres will connect local youth and other job-seekers with all possible job opportunities in a transparent and effective manner through the use of technology as well as through counselling and training. While the state-of-the-art technology driven national career service portal will, in a sustained manner, provide information about available job opportunities and resources for career centres to function effectively, the career centres would be the pivotal outreach and counselling interface of the national career service for teeming millions of aspiring youth from rural, semi-urban areas as well as from disadvantaged sections of the society.

These Centres would be staffed by motivated and competent personnel, enabled with necessary tools and infrastructure for accomplishing the following purposes:

1. Effectively and continuously assessing demand of skills in labour markets, local in other States and abroad.
2. Guiding youth visiting the centres or by outreach to schools/colleges, various training institutions, about the training, on-the-job training, job opportunities etc. according to their aptitude and potential.
3. Connecting youth and other job seekers with jobs through portal, job fairs and other possible interface with employees

such as campus placements.

4. Mobilizing employers and other placement agencies to connect to NCS for meeting their HR requirements.

14.5.2 Services Offered through Career Centres: Career centres will be responsible for all activities related to the NCS project and will be linked to the NCS portal services for improved quality of services and outcomes. Activities to be performed by career centres can be categorized as follows:

A. Coverage (Catchment Area): Each career centre would cater to a catchment area comprising around 3-4 adjacent districts covering an area of approximately 100 square kilometres to map out the availability of institutions, industry, demographics etc. and post the details on the NCS portal for general access. The catchment area is for the purpose of capturing information on the portal in a comprehensive manner and is not intended to deny access of services to any candidate. The Ministry of Labour and Employment would facilitate model career centres in conducting demand and supply assessment survey.

B. Demand Side (Industry Interaction): Career centres will undertake market sizing exercise to estimate the number of employment opportunities in their area, associated skill requirements, skill training capacity availability etc. This will require close and constant interface with local industry and employers.

C. Supply Side (Candidate Engagement): On the supply side, career centres will provide counselling services to the job seekers and make them aware of opportunities based on their skills, area of interest and requirement. Career centres will thus provide a range of employment related services like career counselling, job matching, employment market analytics and other value added services.

D. Job and Skill Mapping: Career centre will undertake the job skill mapping for identification of right fit job for candidate. The candidates will be assessed through skill assessment and psychometric tests and guided to the right opportunity whether it is for employment, skill training, apprenticeship training, on-the-job-training, finishing course (gap training) etc.

E. IEC Activities: Career centre will through multi-pronged IEC strategy increase awareness amongst the various stakeholders like skill training institutes, assessment bodies, schools and college administration, local community leaders, government departments and public in general about the services available.

F. Last Mile Employability Courses: The Ministry is evolving a scheme for offering last mile employability courses for enhancing the employability of youth. These courses will be made available through selected institutions after approval of the scheme and will be rolled out through the model career centres.

15

Internet and Jobs

Internet is a vast and connected network of individual computers and computer networks for the purpose of communicating with each other, using the same communication protocol—transmission control protocol/internet protocol (TCP/IP). When two or more computers are connected a network is created. When two or more networks are connected, an *inter-network* (or internet) is created. The internet, as commonly understood, is the largest example of such a system. Internet is often and aptly described as *information superhighway*, a means to reach innumerable potential destinations. The destination can be any one of the connected networks and host computers.

15.1 Major Uses of Internet

These are the following:

15.1.1 File Transfer Protocol (FTP): It is a mechanism for transferring files between computers on the internet. It is possible to transfer a file to and from a computer (FTP site) without having an account in that machine. Any organization intending to make available to public its documents would normally set up a FTP site from which any one can access the documents for download. Certain FTP sites are available to validated users with an account ID and password.

15.1.2 Electronic-mail (E-mail): The most common and basic use of internet is the exchange of e-mail. It is an extremely powerful and revolutionary result of internet which has facilitated almost instantaneous communication with people in any part of the world. With enhancements like attachment of documents, audio, video and voice mail, this segment of internet is fast expanding as the most used communication medium for the whole world. Many websites offer e-mail as a free facility to individuals. Many corporates have interfaced their private networks with internet in order to make their e-mail accessible from outside their corporate network.

15.1.3 World Wide Web (WWW): Internet encompasses any electronic communication between computers using TCP/IP protocol, such as e-mail, file transfers etc. WWW is a segment of internet, which uses hyper text mark-up language (HTML) to link together files containing text, rich text, sound, graphics, video etc. and offers a very convenient means of navigating through the net. It uses hypertext transfer protocol (HTTP) for communication between computers. Web documents, which are referred to as pages, can contain links to other related documents in a tree like structure. The person browsing one document can access any other linked page. The web documents and the web browsers which are the application programmes to access them, are designed to be platform independent. Thus, any web document can be accessed irrespective of the platform of the computer accessing the document and that of the host computer. The *point and click* method of browsing is extremely simple for any lay user of the net. In fact, the introduction of web since early 1990 has made internet an extremely popular medium and its use in business has been enhanced dramatically.

The next in the HTML genre is the extensible mark-up language (XML), which allows automated two-way information flow between data stores and browser screens. XML documents provide both the raw content of data and the data structure and are projected by its proponents as taking the web technology beyond the limits of HTML.

15.1.4 Wireless Application Protocol (WAP): WAP is the latest industry standard which provides wireless access to internet through hand-held devices like a cellular telephone. This is an open standard promoted by WAP forum and has been adopted by all major handset manufacturers of the world. WAP is supplemented by wireless application environment

(WAE), which provides industry-wise standard for developing applications and services for wireless communication networks. This is based on www technology and provides for application for small screens, with interactive capabilities and adequate security. Wireless transaction protocol (WTP), which is the equivalent of TCP, sets the communication rules and wireless transport layer security (WTLS) provides the required security by encrypting all the session data. WAP is set to revolutionize the commercial use of net.

15.2 Help in Job Search

Internet plays an important role for the job seekers and employers as it has saved the time of both. Job seekers who use the internet have higher probability of being employed. Job search on the internet can definitely serve as a signal. The employers and the job seekers both are proficient in using computers and browsing internet.

15.3 Impact on Earning

People who have access to the new digital technology have benefited in the form of improved employment possibility. Internet use is becoming necessary for certain kinds of social and political participation and for access to some private markets and government services. Technology-linked wage gains show improved productivity due to the use of the new technology at work. Internet use may also contribute to earnings by enhancing access to labour-market information and by serving as a signal of status or competence. Internet can be used as a source of social capital and as a cultural resource. Internet users may benefit from online job listings, expanding personal social network, benefit their employers with useful information, contacting clients or setting up collaborative ventures. Internet users earned more than non-users. The labour market rewarded internet use at home and at work, and workers who went online at home and work did best of all.

15.4 Impact on Professionalism

Traditional concepts of professionalism have been significantly challenged by the appropriation of internet technologies. Some people misuse internet on professional ground because its authenticity cannot be verified. The emergence of new forms of expertise on the internet, by challenging established institutional and professional guarantees of expertise, undermines important and powerful arbiters of ethical forms and behaviours. Convenience, access, and price act as motivators for seeking non-traditional sources of advice and information on the internet. It provides a sense of belonging.

The increasing use of the internet to access knowledge and advice—once thought to be the exclusive province of particular professions—challenges both the meaning of the term profession and the infrastructure assumptions which supports codes of professional conduct. On the other hand, internet can also become a means for professions to successfully negotiate the challenges created by virtual environment. It is concluded that the internet provides a means of reinforcing traditional professional practice, thus increasing the quest for alternative sources of knowledge and information, leading to the pressure for internet regulations on the part of the professions and increasing the quests for alternatives.

15.5 Impact on Labour Market

E-commerce has played an important role to generate employment in economy. This is possible through improved labour facilitation and direct employment for developing countries. The maintenance and supervision of the additional hardware and software systems that are pre-requisites for e-commerce have led to the need of more computer workers. Internet technologies that drive the global information revolution that is happening around have made outsourcing of service-related jobs to developing countries possible. The rise of internet has also led to increase in women's presence in paid employment and has further reduced gender-based discrimination. Internet has positively impacted the labour productivity because e-commerce reduces the co-ordination costs between different work processes, facilitates firms to fragment tasks and thus enables them to improve labour productivity. Development of more interactive job search sites allows job seekers to store search preferences and user profiles and easily follow-up on identified vacancies by making online applications.

Internet is invaluable for employers as well. The ease of posting employment openings, the relatively low cost of advertising and the speed of candidates' response are all positively related to the use of internet. There is also a shift in labour demand towards high-skilled workers, both in manufacturing and non-manufacturing industries.

15.6 Impact on Married Women's Labour Participation

Educated married women with children are actively using internet and there is a large increase in their participation. Internet has saved time and money as it facilitates individual life in different ways. The high-speed internet use has positively impacted the labour supply decisions of married women as it facilitates work-family balance. Tele-work has increased the wages by reducing travel times and by improving productivity through reductions in absenteeism. Effect of high-speed internet on labour supply will be relatively more positive for married women than single women and men if the internet is used for tele-work and home production.

Bibliography

Bibliography

Anand Singh, K. and Krishna, K.V.S.M. (1994), "Agricultural Entrepreneurship: The Concept and Evidence", *Journal of Entrepreneurs*, Vol. 3, No. 1, March.

Arnold, V.D. and Roach, T.D. (1989), "Teaching: A Non-verbal Communication Event", *Business Education Forum,* 44, 18-20.

Arora, R. and Sood, S.K. (2007), "Fundamentals of Entrepreneurship and Small Business", in Baporikar, N. (ed.), 'Entrepreneurship Development and Project Management', Himalaya Publication House, New Delhi.

Arvinda, Ch. (2001), "Women Entrepreneurs: An Exploratory Study", Public Opinion Survey, Indian Institute of Public Opinion, New Delhi.

Beena, C. and Sushma, B. (2003), "Women Entrepreneurs Managing Petty Business: A Study from Motivational Perspective", *Southern Economist*, Vol. 42, May.

Bhalla, Sheila (2008), "Definitional and Statistical Issues Relating to Workers in Informal Employment", National Commission for Enterprises in the Unorganised Sector (NCEUS), New Delhi, Working Paper No. 3.

Bhanushali, S.G. (1987), "Entrepreneurship Development", Himalaya Publishing House, New Delhi.

Blaug, M. (1973), "Education and the Employment Problem in Developing Countries", International Labour Organization, Geneva.

Central Board of Secondary Education (1997), "Value Education: A Handbook for Teachers", New Delhi.

Chakrabarti, M. (2004), "Value Education: Changing Perspectives", Kanishka Publishers, New Delhi.

Chandra Lekha, R.S. (1995), "Value Education for College Students", *University News*, Association of Indian Universities, New Delhi.

Chandra, Kohil Shanta (1991), "Development of Women Entrepreneurship in India", Mittal Publications, New Delhi.

Choudhury, P.K., Shashi, Baijal and Asokan, M. (1997), "Bank and Women Enterprise Development: A Comparison of Approaches in India and UK", SEDME, XXIV, National Institute of Micro,

Small and Medium Enterprises.

Deshpande, M.U. (1984), "Entrepreneurship of Small-scale Industries", Deep and Deep Publication, New Delhi.

Dhameja S.K., Bhatia, B.S. and Saini, J.S. (2000), "Women Entrepreneurs: Their Perceptions about Business Opportunities and Attitudes towards Entrepreneurial Support Agencies", SEDME, 27/4, National Institute of Micro, Small and Medium Enterprises.

Dreze, J. and Sen, A. (1996), "India: Economic Development and Social Opportunity", Oxford University Press, New Delhi.

Dubhashi, P.R (1994), "Indian System of Higher Education", *University News*, February.

Government of India, Ministry of Finance, *Economic Survey* (various years).

—Planning Commission, Report of the Working Group on Skill Development and Vocational Training, 2006.

Goyal, Meenu and Parkash, Jai (2011), "Women Entrepreneurship in India: Problems and Prospects", *International Journal of Multidisciplinary Research*, Vol. 1, Issue 5, September.

Joshi, S.M. and Biswal, A. (2002), "Taming the Information and Communication Technology for Teacher Education", *University News*, July 15-21, Vol. 40, No. 28.

Kirve, P. and Kanitkar, M. (1993), "Entrepreneurship at the Grassroots: Developing the Income Generating Capabilities of Rural Women", *Journal of Entrepreneurship*, Vol. 2, No. 1, July.

Kulkarni, Manu N. (1996), "Evolving a Women's Policy", *Economic and Political Weekly*, Vol. 31, No. 12, March 23.

Kumar S. (2001), "Development of Scale for Rating Teaching Performance of the University Teachers by Their Students", Centre for Advanced Studies in Education, The Maharaja Sayyaji Rao University of Baroda, Vadodara.

Leo, Paul Dona (1993), "Environment for Entrepreneurship: A Model of Public Policy and Economic Development", *The Journal of Entrepreneur*, Vol. 2, No. 1, September.

Mahanty, Sangram Keshari (2005), "Fundamentals of Entrepreneurship", Prentice Hall of India, New Delhi.

Mehta, Aasha Kapur (1996), "Recasting Indices for Developing Countries: A Gender Empowerment Measure", *Economic and Political Weekly*, Vol. 31, No. 43, October.

Panandikar, Surekha (1985), "Women Entrepreneurs: Problems and Potentials", *Economic Times*, December 26.

Pattanaik, Bikram K. (1997), "Empowerment of Women and Rural Development", *Yojana*, Vol. 41, No. 10, October.

Pillai, Jaya Kothai (1995), "Women and Empowerment", Gyan Publishing House, New Delhi.

Rani (1986), "Potential Women Entrepreneurs: A Study", SEDME, 13(3), National Institute of Micro, Small and Medium Enterprises.

Rao, Harinarayana (1991), "Promotion of Women Entrepreneurship", SEDME, 18(2), National Institute of Micro, Small and Medium Enterprises, March.

Reddy, J. Suresh (2004), "Entrepreneurship: Concept and Development", *Third Concept*, Vol. 17, June-August.

Scarpetta, S., Pages, C. and Pierre, G. (2008), "Job Creation in Latin America and the Caribbean", World Bank, Washington D.C.

Singh, Kamala (1992), "Women Entrepreneurs", Ashish Publishing House, New Delhi.

Tilak, J.B.G. (2002), "Vocational Education and Training in Asia", in John P. Keeves and Rye Watanabe (eds.), 'The Handbook on Educational Research in the Asia-Pacific Region', Kluwer Academic Publishers.

Tulus, Tambunan (2009), "Women Entrepreneurship in Asian Developing Countries: Their Development and Main Constraints", *Journal of Development and Agricultural Economics,* Vol. 1, No. 2, May.

Udaykumar, M.A. and Sreehdhara, T.N (2002), "Entrepreneurship Development Programmes: An Analysis", *Southern Economist*, Vol. 54, May.

Udaykumar, M.A. (2002), "Entrepreneurship Development Programmes (EDPs) and the Development of Entrepreneurs: A Study", *Small Enterprise Development Management Extension*, Vol. 29, No. 4, April.

UNESCO (1998), "World Education Report: Teachers and Teaching in a Changing World", UNESCO, Paris.

Vasanthakumari, P. (2012), "Economic Empowerment of Women through Micro Enterprises in India with Special Reference to Promotional Agencies", *International Journal of Multidisciplinary Research*, Vol. 2, No.1, January.

Vinze, Megha Dubhashi (1987), "Women Entrepreneurs in India: A

Socio-economic Study of Delhi", Mittal Publications, Delhi.
World Bank (1995), "Investing in Young Children", World Bank Discussion Paper 275, Washington D.C.
World Bank (2007), "Cultivating Knowledge and Skills to Grow African Agriculture", Washington D.C.

Websites

Ministry of Skill Development and Entrepreneurship
Ministry of Human Resource Development
Ministry of Labour and Employment
Ministry of Micro, Small and Medium Enterprises
Ministry of Social Justice and Empowerment

Index

Index